SCRÍBHINNÍ BÉALOIDIS

FOLKLORE STUDIES

2

ALL IN! ALL IN!

A SELECTION OF DUBLIN CHILDREN'S TRADITIONAL
STREET-GAMES WITH RHYMES AND MUSIC

EILÍS BRADY

Comhairle Bhéaloideas Éireann
An Coláiste Ollscoile

Baile Átha Cliath
1984
Dublin

© Comhairle Bhéaloideas Éireann

Printed in the Republic of Ireland by
The Leinster Leader Ltd., Naas
for the publishers:

Comhairle Bhéaloideas Éireann
University College
Belfield
Dublin 4

Acknowledgements

I wish to thank Tomás de Bhaldraithe, who first suggested that I should record the street-games of my neighbourhood, for his constant advice and encouragement.

My thanks are also due to Eileen Bhreathnach for transcribing the music from tape and Austin Bevan for preparing it for the blockmakers, and to Fergus Bourke, Bill Doyle, G. A. Duncan, Austin Finn, Liam Ó Cuanaigh and Patrick Peacock whose photographs add greatly to the book. I am also indebted to Mary Bergin, Breandán Breathnach, Vera Fitzpatrick, Meta Gale, Kathleen Gallagher, Gifford Lewis, May McGrath, Caoimhín Ó Marcaigh and Peter Slattery and to the reading-room staff of the National Library for their assistance. Without the sympathetic co-operation of Mr. W. Britton and the staff of the Leinster Leader this book could never have been published.

I am especially grateful to Comhairle Bhéaloideas Éireann for the inclusion of my book in its series and to the editor of the series, Professor Bo Almqvist, who scrutinized my manuscript and read all the proofs.

This is in all essentials a reprint of the 1975 hard back edition. Minor corrections have been made.

Contents

INTRODUCTION ... ... xiii–xv

BACKGROUND LANGUAGE 1–3

TAKING NOTICE 4–13
Cook 5. Clap hands 5. One potato 5. Bum, bum, bailey-o 6. Round and round the garden 6. This is the way 6. Shake hands brother 6. This little piggy 7. Dandling rhymes 7. Johnny Wetbread 7. Rosie Apple 9. Johnny Magory 9. Supposing, supposing 9. Punch and Judy 10. Swinging on a gate 10. Paddy on the railway 11. Ring-a-ring-a-rosie 12. Sally go round the moon 12. Jinny go up 13. Yip, yip, a nanny-goat 13. Windy weather 13.

WORDS AT WILL 14–23
Jeering 14. The chance to chant 17. Ritual 20. Spin, spout, or . . . 20. Rain, rain, come down 21. Pie, pie, come out 21. Shut your eyes 21. Curtness 22. Superstitions 22. See a pin 22. My straw bamer 23. The banshee 23.

PURE DEVILMENT 24–26
A run-away knock 24. Boxing the fox 24. Scutting 25. Swinging on a lamp-post 25.

MAKE-BELIEVE 27–29

Playing house 27. Playing mothers 28. Playing shop 29.

SIMPLE PLEASURES 30–35

Stilts 30. A peep-show 31. Working with wool 31. Jinny-Joe's eggs 32. Catching bees 32. Do you like butter? 33. One o'clock 33. It will, it won't 33. Hell, Heaven, Purgatory or Limbo 33. Badges 33. Comb and paper 34. A Buzz 34. A leg and a duck 34. Shake the blanket 34. Carry a lady to London 34. Jack, Jack 35. King of the castle 35.

DEXTERITY 36–47

Hot hands 36. Chestnuts 38. Mowl 38. Five slates 39. Jackstones 39. Spinning a top 44. Rolling your hoop 46.

PICKING SIDES 48–52

BALL GAMES 53–68

Hopping a ball 53. Playing ball against a wall 61. Queenie 67. Donkey 68.

SKIPPING 69–99

Chase, chase 71. Drip drop 72. Flowers 72. Salt, mustard 78. I call in 78. Bluebells 83. Action rhymes 84. German boys 87. Handy Andy 87. Up the ladder 88. Ee-ver, eye-ver 88. A change of tune 90. Apple jelly 90. Down by the river 91. All in together 95. French skipping 99. Jumps 99.

PORTRAITS OF LIFE 100–129

The farmer wants a wife 101. Stands a lady 102. The old woman from Sandy Land 105. Here's the gipsy riding 106. The King of rifles 109. Chinese Governor 110. Will you marry 110. The Roman Soldiers 112. All around the village 115. I sent a letter 116. Wallflowers, wallflowers 117. Old Roger is dead 118. In and out through the darkie bluebells 120. Lazy Mary 121. Oosha Mary Murphy 123. Little Mary 123. Dear Anne 123. There was a girl in our school 124. When I was a . . . 126. The dummy's band 127. The wee Polony man 127. Dancing up the highway 128.

FROM KERB TO KERB 130–133

Evens and odds 130. Traffic lights 131. Bread and water 131. Cock-cock-a-rooshy 131. Johnny may I go across the water? 132. Giant steps 132. Uncles and aunts 133. Sally-o 133.

GOOD V. EVIL 134–138

Statues 134. Monday, Tuesday 135. I'm stirring my chicken 135. Ghost in the garden 136. Good Angel, bad angel 137. Colours 138.

STRENGTH 139–141

Red rover 139. Half of the castle 139. Here's the robbers passing by 140.

GUESSING GAMES 142–143

Towns and counties 142. O'clock 142. Woolworth's 143. Television ads 143.

CHASING 144–150

Tip and tig 144. Sticky apple 144. Duck chasing 144. I've no iron 145. Follow the arrow 145. Kick the can 146. Relieve-ee-o 146. Hide and go seek 147. Witches 148. Catching in the rope 148. Colour chasing 148. Mr. Fox 149. Old Granny Grey 149. Old Daddy Aiken 150.

MARBLES 151–152

Taw the hole 151. Sticking in 152. Follow 152. Fives 152.

BEDS 153–159

Pickey beds 153. Name beds 155. Roundy beds 156. Aeroplane beds 157. French beds 158. Ball beds 159.

MISCELLANEOUS GAMES 160–166

Snap the bacon 160. O'Grady says 160. The cat and the mouse 161. Pussy four corners 161. Ball between the feet 161. Granny went to market 161. The big ship sails 162. Sew, sew, sew 162. I spy . . . 163. Did you ever 164. Hop, hop, to the baker's shop 164. Long or short 165. Dublin, Derry, Cork, Kerry 166.

ix

VARIOUS VERSES 167–177

The waxies' dargle 167. Cheer boys cheer 168. Down in the alley-o 169. I've a pain in my belly 170. Down by the river Sawl-ya 170. Janey Mac 171. I have a gumboil 172. Proddy Woddy on the wall 172. If a gumboil 172. If-ika-you-ika 172. I see Paris 173. How is your old one 173. Oh! the horse broke down 174. Round apple 174. . . . sells fish 176. Cheer up . . . 176.

CLASSIFIED INDEX 179–192

INDEX OF FIRST LINES 193–195

Illustrations

1. Wallflowers, wallflowers. Photo: Eilís Brady.
2. So turn your back against the game. Photo: Eilís Brady.
3. A hoop my be seen parked . . . Photo: Eilís Brady.
4. Queenie eye-o. Photo: Eilís Brady.
5. Being well away from main-road traffic this road is safe for skipping. Photo: Eilís Brady.
6. Die die little dog die. Photo: Eilís Brady.
7. They will always prefer the thrills and excitement of swinging on a lamp-post. Photo: Patrick Peacock.
8. Performing all sorts of acrobatic feats like the *duck*. Photo: Patrick Peacock.
9. Swinging in a different setting. Photo: Austin Finn.
10. In the shadow of the Black Church. Photo: Courtesy of Bord Fáilte Éireann.
11. Getting a shove off. Photo: Fergus Bourke.
12. Hopping on one foot she kicks the pickey from bed to bed never letting down the other foot. Photo: Patrick Peacock.
13. The number of boys to be seen playing beds has increased considerably. Photo: Eilís Brady.
14. An empty shoe-polish or ointment tin makes an ideal pickey. Photo: Bill Doyle.
15. DONKEY. Photo: Eilís Brady.
16. Ready-made shop toys play no part in these street-games. Photo: Liam Ó Cuanaigh.

17. Ring-a-ring-a-rosie. Photo: Eilís Brady.
18. A-sha, a-sha, we all fall down. Photo: Eilís Brady.
19. When you have no front gate you swing from your Georgian doorway. Photo: Courtesy of the *Irish Press*.
20. In fact a swing can be erected anywhere. Photo: Fergus Bourke.
21. Jumps. Photo: Bill Doyle.
22. Standing hopefully by helping to swing the rope. Photo: G. A. Duncan.
23. Once there is chalk to be had no surface escapes. Photo: Courtesy of Roinn Bhéaloideas Éireann.
24. Mowl. Photo: Liam Ó Cuanaigh.
25. Lifting open the small cover of the water hydrant and aiming coins into it. Photo: Bill Doyle.
26. The amount of concentration spent on each throw is amazing. Photo: Liam Ó Cuanaigh.
27. A player may land his coin directly into the mowl. Photo: Liam Ó Cuanaigh.
28. Scut the whip! Photo: Bill Doyle.
29. Then they may run off to the newsagents and knock down the placards outside. Photo: Courtesy of the *Irish Times*.
30. If she can get old high-heeled shoes so much the better. Photo: Liam Ó Cuanaigh.
31. I call in. Photo: G. A. Duncan.
32. Jackstones. Photo: Fergus Bourke.
33. Very young children are specially cherished. Photo: Courtesy of the *Irish Times*.
34. Picking sides. Photo: Eilís Brady.

All the photographs were taken in Dublin, most of them in the past three years.

Cover photograph by Liam Ó Cuanaigh.

Introduction

Old Dublin, that is the Dublin of the tenements and the back-streets, is fast disappearing. Whole areas are being cleared out and the families re-settled in large housing estates in the suburbs. This has been going on for the past forty years. It would be a mistake to think that because of this change, the speech and the street-games of these areas are lost forever. Certainly, they are lost forever from the city area that has been cleared, but if you follow the families out to the suburbs you will find the speech and the street-games flourishing more than ever in their new surroundings; especially the street-games, because usually the roads of a large housing estate, being well away from main-road traffic, are safer for playing games than the streets in the city centre where the families come from. I said 'especially the street-games'— because the speech does undergo a certain change in the new surroundings.

Now, when each family has a house of its own, the old accom-modation in *front parlour* or *back parlour, front drawing-room* or *back drawing-room, two pair back* or *two pair front, top back* or *top front* becomes only a memory, and the words go from usage to be replaced by words like *front gate, back gate, front garden, back garden, bathroom, bedroom* and *sitting-room. Streets, Lanes, Places,* and *Squares* give way to *Roads, Avenues, Drives,* and *Terraces.* Apart from these various word differences very little else changes. The accent and the speech patterns remain the same, and the children from the various areas of the city come together in the suburbs bringing with them their games and rhymes and very distinctive speech.

A typical example of this type of housing estate is The Park, where I grew up and where I still live. It is the centre circle of a small scheme of Corporation[1] houses built before the last war, and is within half an hour's walk from the city centre. The Park consists of fifty-four houses surrounding a sort of village green. Being away from main-road traffic, it has always been an ideal place for children to play.

Originally, half of the tenants were people who had been living in overcrowded or condemned areas in the city, and for whom these houses were primarily built. The other half were people who had been purchasing houses from the Corporation in suburbs like Inchicore, Drumcondra, Fairview and Marino and who, finding themselves unable to afford them, surrendered them back to the Corporation (without any financial compensation) in exchange for these smaller and cheaper houses.

No conventional playground could ever provide as much enjoyment as The Park does. There are lamp-posts to swing on, walls to play ball against, grass to lie on, gardens to hide in, hedges to hide behind, steps to sit on, and always some neighbour's new baby to wheel around.

There is a constant seventy to eighty children living in The Park. This ensures the continuance of the street-games and rhymes and very colourful language as an integral part of the life there. At the moment, twenty-two of the fifty-four families have young children, some of school-going age. An interesting and very important thing about the parents is their continuing custom of sending the children to different schools. One reason for this is that parents like to send their children to whatever school they themselves attended, if this is at all possible. Another reason is the simple one of striving for individuality where possible. We are very fortunate in having a variety of schools within a radius of about one mile of The Park, so you find the children going to about ten different schools. This is vitally important for children whose houses are so close to each other. It means that it is as real playmates they come together out of doors to enjoy their street-games.

When I decided to set down these games and rhymes it was not very difficult for me to become, as it were, 'tuned in' to all those sounds that create the special atmosphere of The Park. All I had

---

[1] The administrative authority in Dublin is called the Corporation.

to do was observe (unobtrusively) and listen as the children, at the first hint of Spring, cast down the toys bought for them at Christmas, and came out to play in the open air—out to play all the games I knew so well. I noticed how little the games and rhymes had changed since I played here, the tunes remained exactly the same. This may, perhaps, be due to the fact that it is the children themselves who hand on the games to the younger ones. It is a familiar sight to see a game in progress and two or three prams with infants in them parked close by, the infants alert and responsive to the gaiety and excitement. Toddlers are encouraged to join in a game whenever possible; older children take a special delight in initiating them into the intricacies of the various games.

A great many of the games are accompanied by a variety of verses and some of these verses are chanted to quite distinctive tunes. Now that I have become conscious of them, these tunes seem to fill the air with an atmosphere of eternal youth.

I have set down here the games and rhymes which I have played myself in The Park and which are still being played there. I have also included those games which are no longer played and new ones which have been accepted by the children and become part of their repertoire. That is not to say that these games are not also played elsewhere, either exactly as I have described them here or in variant forms.

The local pronunciation is very distinctive. It could not be adequately described here without the use of phonetic symbols. I have therefore used standard spelling throughout.

Background Language

An important part of the atmosphere of The Park is created by the language of the mothers towards the children. Generally, this language is used publicly either directly at the children or to other mothers about the children. It is usually extravagantly critical, but never consciously hurtful.

The children are well used to being chastised and kept in their places by neighbours whom they may have annoyed no less than by their own mothers. And it's not hard to annoy neighbours or parents who have children *like steps of stairs*. So we have all at some time been called *a big baa* when we cried over something trivial, or were told unsympathetically *The bladder was near your eye*. The peevish, whinging, child who *wouldn't be happy in God's pocket* is *crying someone out of the house*. The idea here is that the child is like the banshee (Irish: *bean sí,* fairy woman) who is often heard crying in the night before a death. The neighbours will be told *She's like a bag of cats all day Missus, I can't stir for her! She's under my feet all day! She's after my heels all day!* They in turn will then take up the chorus with another neighbour *That child's a real ma's plaster! You can't look crooked at that child or she'll cry!* No, the whinge is definitely not tolerated by anyone. And it is useless to complain of an odd pain or an ache, you'll be told unsympathetically *It's far from your arse you won't sit on it!* or *You'll be better before you're twice married!*

ALL IN! ALL IN!

Someone may say in praise of a neighbour's child *You'd steal her!*
You'd run away with her! She's a conny little thing! Yet nobody
would hesitate to call a bold, vindictive, thwarting, child (no
matter how pretty), be it their own or a neighbour's, *a bugger,*
a canat (ca nat), a faggot, a get, a get of hell, a (bloody) persecuting
little get, a bloody little sleeveen get, a heart-scald (because he would
have your heart scalded); *a bloody little scut.* They'll warn such a
child threateningly *Ah then, if I catch you! If I lay my hands on you!*
Wait till your father comes in! Wait till your father goes out! Get
to hell's gates out of that! I'll take your sacred life! I'll redden your
arse for you! You want a bloody good skelp on th'arse to straighten
you (and I'll give it to you)! A mother may even be forced to admit
to a neighbour *He'll get me taken one of these days!* (he'll go too
far and I'll have to go to court to answer for him).

Now it's bad enough to be bold but it's much worse to be *a*
crab—old beyond your years and usually of small build. *It's no*
wonder she can't grow she's too crabby they say of such a child,
who will also be called *a ferret* or described as *ferrety-faced* or
having *a farthing face* or, most cutting of all, *a little sparrow-fart.*
Then, there's another word for such a child—an old *grannuaile*[1]—
(pronounced *granya wail*). It's only the ·suggestion of the word
'granny' in this that makes it sound appropriate.

Whenever there is any appreciation of an unusually perceptive
child, you'll hear *That child is not right!* or *That child was here*
before! or *That child was on the world before!* and although it is
said jokingly, there is an implication of some fairy influence at work.

A child won't be allowed to listen to the conversation of grown-
ups, she's told *Get to hell's gates out from under my feet and*
don't be up in people's mouths like that—eating the business (taking
in all that's being said) because you have to watch your words *on*
(in) front of children or *they'd hang you!* If a child does chime
into a conversation she'll be smartly discouraged with *Listen to*

---

[1] *Grannuaile* is the popular anglicized form of the name of one of Ireland's
most colourful women of the sixteenth century—it is a corruption of her Irish
name, Gráinne Ní Mháille. She was born in 1530 and spent most of her childhood
on Clare Island in Clew Bay on the west coast of Ireland. Her father was an Irish
Chieftain and sea-captain who owned extensive lands in Connacht. Gráinne
inherited her father's love of the sea and later inherited his trading fleet and
became one of the most renowned sea-captains of the time. She married an
O'Flaherty of Galway in 1550 and had three sons. Down the years so much
romance surrounded the story of Grannuaile and her exploits on land and sea
that in modern times she became an almost legendary figure; but she also became
the personification of resurgent Ireland in songs like *Óró 'Sé Do Bheatha Abhaile*
and *O'Donovan Rossa's Farewell to Dublin.*

ninety-eight and boney! Old ninety-eight in the shade! The child asking *Where's Mammy?* will be told *She's gone off with a soldier! She's gone off with a highlander!*

Children must never mimic the physical defects of others because *mocking is catching.* And if you happen to remark to a mother that her child is a fine child or pretty—always remember to add God's blessing. *She has beautiful eyes, God bless them!* Because if anything were to happen to the child's eyes, your omission would be remembered and how you might have put your *unlucky eye* on the child. Most parents just want to have all their children *on the baker's list,* even if this means *they'd eat you out of house and home,* or *they'd eat the forehead off you—there's no filling them.* The child who can't finish his dinner having asked for too much in the first place, is told *Your eyes were bigger than your belly.*

Such critical and extravagant comments must amaze and dismay the outsider. But this language is in keeping with the tendency to exaggerate and overstate which is characteristic of the Dublin dialect. The children are never distressed by this language, in fact *it rolls off them like water off a duck's back.* Because, while the words used are at times excessive, the tone of their delivery is usually one of mock exasperation, intended to impress the neighbours as much as to chastise the child.

Inside the home a different note is struck. *A scut,* and *a get,* a child may be called in front of the neighbours, but in the privacy of the home that child experiences the warm affection of its parents, expressed in different though no less characteristic terms. Here, a little girl can bask in the security of being *her Daddy's little hen,* or his *little granny hen,* or his *little bunser.* And there's a world of affection in being called *her Mammy's one star of hope!* or *a lovely girl, fit for an earl!* If an unpleasant task must be done, like dressing a wound, the child is reassured and comforted by the words *I wouldn't hurt you—not for the world and Garrett Reilly!* So, the harshness of the language used towards them in public is balanced out by the affection they experience in the home.

Taking Notice

Infants and very young children are specially cherished by everyone. Older children[1] lavish the same care and affection on them as their parents do. Teaching a small child to walk is a great joy to all.[2] Seldom, if ever, will you see a reins used as a walking-aid, a child is always taken by the hand. Amusing them and encouraging them *to take notice* is a great source of satisfaction to parents and older children. This is done by teaching them very simple games. It will be noticed that in these games no toys are used. Instead, the child is made aware of its hands, fingers, open palm, closed fist, face and toes. The simple rhymes which accompany the actions of each game are easily learned and identified by the child. These games may be played in the house with parents and older brothers and sisters or out of doors when the infant is being 'minded' by an older child. By their very nature these simple amusements establish a close bond between the infants and young children and their parents and older children. Thus, the child experiences from its earliest days the warmth of human contact. This contact is continued in the street-games when the child is brought into the charmed circle of such games as *Wallflowers* and *The Farmer Wants a Wife* by the older children. When a child is identified

[1] These are usually girls of twelve to fourteen years, though not necessarily related to the young children. It is quite common for a girl of this age to 'adopt' a neighbour's young child and take care of it as though she were it's older sister.

[2] See p. 9 *Rosie Apple*.

4

as 'the youngest child' in *Wallflowers* and has his (or her) name called out, this gives him a great sense of his importance to the game, and also a sense of fellowship with the other children.

It would be difficult (and perhaps inaccurate) to equate a certain age-group with certain games. *Paddy on the Railway, Yip, Yip, a Nanny-goat*, and *Swinging on a Gate*, are the province of very young children and toddlers, whom you will also find amusing themselves with their own versions of the games and rhymes of the older children.

COOK

This is in fact the most elementary form of hide-and-seek. Having first caught the child's attention, you then place your two hands over your face and say *Cook!* Then you slowly part your two hands to reveal your face—much to the delight of the child. It is surprising how quickly the child then goes on to part your two hands himself, and so, he has learned his first game. *Hide-and-seek* is often called *Cook* because *Cook!* is sometimes the signal given that everyone is in hiding and the search may begin.

CLAP HANDS

Teaching an infant to *clap hands* is accompanied by this little verse:

> Clap hands, clap hands,
> Till Daddy comes home,
> Cake in his pocket
> For (*Name*) alone.

ONE POTATO

This is played with the fists which are supposed to be potatoes. At each number you place a fist on top of the one before you, it always ends in laughter and confusion.

> One potato,
> Two potato,
> Three potato, four.
> Five potato,
> Six potato,
> Seven potatoes more.

5

BUM, BUM, BAILEY-O

This is another verse which can be used with the previous game:

> Bum, bum, bailey-o,
> Two to one a nailey-o.
> Barbel-ee, barbel-o,
> Bum, bum, bailey-o.

ROUND AND ROUND THE GARDEN

You take the child's hand and go gently round the palm with your index finger. Then 'one step, two steps' are taken along the arm with the index and middle fingers alternatively, ending under the armpit with a tickle.

> Round and round the garden,
> I lost my teddy bear.
> One step, two steps,
> And a tickly under there.

THIS IS THE WAY

One child extends her bare arm palm upwards while another child (or an adult) goes gently up and down the arm with the tips of her fingers, saying the verse, ending under the armpit causing much laughter.

> This is the way my father showed me
> How to play the fiddle.
> Upstairs, downstairs,
> Especially in the middle.

SHAKE HANDS BROTHER

When an older child is teaching a baby how to shake hands she takes its hand and says:

> Shake hands brother,
> You're a rogue
> And I'm another.
> You stole meat,
> I stole bone,
> You'll go to hell,
> And I'll go home.

THIS LITTLE PIGGY

This little rhyme is said while counting out an infant's toes.

> This little piggy went to the market,
> This little piggy stayed at home,
> This little piggy got bread and butter,
> This little piggy got none.
> Grunt, grunt, grunt, went this little piggy,
> All, all, all, the way home.

DANDLING RHYMES

These rhymes can be used by either mother or father, older brother or sister, to amuse the younger children. You take the child on your lap facing you and place your two arms around it, so that the child can lean its back securely against your hands. Then, while saying the rhyme, you rock the child backwards and forwards until the last word is reached. At the last word, you open your knees so that the child thinks he's going to fall and jerks forward quickly to be hugged in a warm embrace.

> See-saw, maggoty daw,
> Sold her bed to lie in the straw.
> Wasn't she the dirty slut,
> To go and do a thing like that.
> ——◇——
> What's your name?
> Butter and cream[1],
> All the way
> From Dirty Lane[2].
> (or from Cole's Lane)

JOHNNY WETBREAD

Dirty Lane is also mentioned in the following dandling rhyme which has a very interesting background. Oddly enough it was only used by grandmothers or old people when dandling a child. The rhyme itself is seldom heard nowadays, but the name Johnny Wetbread is in common use as a term of unmalicious mockery for a man.

---

[1] Pronounced *crame* to rhyme with *name*.
[2] Now Bridgefoot Street.

ALL IN! ALL IN!

In the dirty end of Dirty Lane
There lived a cobbler Dick McClane.
He wore a coat of the old King's reign,
And so did Johnny Wetbread.

Johnny Wetbread was an old beggarman who used to stand outside the Franciscan Church in Church Street about a hundred years ago. He'd have a bag of crusts and before eating them he'd dip each one in the fountain which was in front of the Church at the time. The original verse was composed by a famous Dublin ballad singer named Michael Moran, nicknamed Zozimus.[1] He was born in the Liberties around 1790 and was blind almost from birth. He earned a living by singing and composing ballads and entertaining the crowds who gathered round him whenever he took up his stand at a street corner. One of his most famous stories was called Zozimus, hence his nickname. Zozimus was a bishop sent by God to hear the confession of a repentent prostitute called Mary of Egypt, and his listeners never tired of hearing the story recounted to them. It began:

> The Imperial throne when Theodosius held
> In Palestine a holy hermit dwelled,
> Whose shining virtues and extensive fame,
> The world astonished—Zozimus his name.

A contemporary of Moran's was a cobbler named Dick McClane whom Moran despised and consequently composed the following verse about him.

> At the dirty end of Dirty Lane
> Lived a dirty cobbler, Dick McClane.
> His wife was in the old King's reign
> A stout brave orange-woman.
> On Essex Bridge she strained her throat,
> And six a penny was her note.
> But Dick he wore a brand-new coat
> He got among the yeomen.
> He was a bigot, like his clan,
> And in the streets he wildly sang
> O toly, toly, toly raid, with his old jade.

—◆—

[1] See 'Memoir of The Great Original Zozimus (Michael Moran)'. The celebrated Dublin street rhymer and reciter. By Gulielmus Dubliniensis Humoriensis. Dublin 1871.

1. Wallflowers, wallflowers (p. 117)
2. So turn your back against the game (p. 118)

3. A hoop may be seen parked ... (p. 47)
4. Queenie eye-o (p. 67)

5. Being well away from main-road traffic this road is safe for skipping (p. 1)

6. Die, die, little dog, die (p. 11)

Dicky, Dicky, Dout,
With his shirt hanging out,
Four yards in,
And four yards out.

That little dandling rhyme is also called after a boy to make him turn and chase you.

ROSIE APPLE

The following dandling rhyme is also used for encouraging a child to take its first steps alone. An older child stands the little one a few paces away from her while saying the verse. Then bending forward with outstretched arms towards the child she repeats the last word: *alone-y, lone-y, lone-y.* With this encouragement the child bravely totters forward into the outstretched and welcoming arms, to be hoisted up in the air *with an Oosha!*[1]

Rosie apple, went to chapel,
Riding on a pony.
Get two sticks and knock her down,
And make her stand alone-y.

JOHNNY MAGORY

Every child loves a story and the smaller ones never cease to respond to the following little verse:

I'll tell you a story
About Johnny Magory.[2]
Will I begin it? Yes!
That's all that's in it.

SUPPOSING, SUPPOSING

Children always respond with expectation to the next two verses while knowing well what's coming at the end:

[1] The words *With an Oosha!* or simply *Oosha!* usually accompanies the action of hoisting a child in the air. It is really an exclamation, and it is also used when children holding hands form a circle, and then decide to close in together towards the centre. They shout a long-drawn-out *Oosha!* as they close in. It also accompanies a girl's name in such verses as *Oosha Mary Murphy!* and *Sally Go Round the Moon.*

[2] A *Johnny Magory* (from the Irish *mucóir*) is the berry of the wild rose.

ALL IN! ALL IN!

Supposing, supposing,
Three men were frozen.
Two died,
How many were left?
'One'
No, None,
'Cause you're only supposing.

PUNCH AND JUDY

Punch and Judy ran a race.
Judy stopped to tie her lace.
Who won?
'Punch!'

For this answer the child gets a gentle 'punch' on the nose.

SWINGING ON A GATE

Children from about three to seven years (boys and girls) love a swing slung between the supports of their own front gate. Apart from the actual pleasure of swinging, they have the sense of security that playing so close to home gives to a small child, and also the sense of freedom that goes with being 'out playing'. A great deal of pleasure too is derived from the preparation of the swing. The very young ones may have it set up for them by a mother or older sister, but they always adjust it themselves to their own liking. If a double strand of rope is used, one strand may be raised higher than the other to serve as a back-support, so that it is quite safe. A cardigan or coat may be folded up to make a comfortable seat. Another child may stand hopefully by helping to swing the rope to and fro and singing:

5, 10, 15, 20,
25, 30, 35, 40,
45, 50, 55, 60,
65, 70, 75, 80,
85, 90, 95, 100.
With a high swing,
And a low swing,
And a swing
To get off of your
Swing, swong, sway.

The last three lines usually have to be repeated many times before she gets off to give the other child a chance, because she is after all swinging from her *own* gate and is very conscious of this. The following rhyme is also used for swinging on a gate.

Die, die, little dog die.
Die for the sake of
Your grandmother's eye.
With a high swing,
And a low swing,
And a swing
To get off of your
Swing, swong, sway.

However, if two or three more children come along and decide to play *Paddy on the Railway* or *Ring-a-ring-a-rosie*, the swing will be hastily undone and the rope thrown into the garden.

PADDY ON THE RAILWAY

The children (boys and girls) holding hands, move around in a circle singing the verse. They go progressively faster like a train.

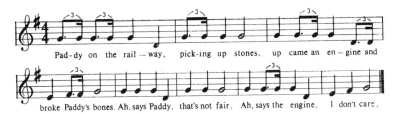

Paddy on the railway,
Picking up stones.
Up came an engine,
And broke Paddy's bones.
Ah, says Paddy,
That's not fair.
Ah, says the engine,
I don't care.

——◆——

Paddy on the railway,
Picking up stones.
Along came an Indian,
And chopped off his nose.
Ah, says Paddy,
That's not fair.
Ah, says the Indian,
I don't care.

RING-A-RING-A-ROSIE

This is done much slower than the verse above, but in the end all
fall down together.

Ring-a-ring-a Ro-sie, a   pocket-ful of po-sies. A-sha, a-sha, we   all fall down.

Ring-a-ring-a-rosie,
A pocket (*or* a bottle) full of posies,
A-sha, a-sha,
We all fall down!

SALLY GO ROUND THE MOON

Young children go round in a circle holding hands singing:

Sally go round the moon,
Sally go round the stars,
Sally go round the chimney pot,
And an Oosha Mary Ann.

JINNY GO UP

> Jinny go up,
> Jinny go down,
> Jinny go all around the town.

YIP, YIP, A NANNY-GOAT

Young children run along in single line each holding the 'tail' (the hem of the coat or dress) of the child in front and sing:

> Yip, yip, a nanny-goat,
> Yip, yip, away.
> When we get our holidays
> We'll all run away.

WINDY WEATHER

This is like *Paddy on the Railway*—all hold hands and at the words 'when the wind blows' they go much faster and usually end up in a heap.

Win-dy weather, fros-ty weather, when the wind blows we all go to-ge—ther.

> Windy weather,
> Frosty weather.
> When the wind blows,
> We all go together.

Words at Will

Surrounded as they are by such a flow of colourful language, it is small wonder that jeering, name-calling, and quick-witted remarks have such a special place among the various amusements of both boys and girls from around seven to thirteen years. Their games are often interrupted by (at times) deliberate outbursts of verbal exchanges—sharp and curt, taunting and challenging; each one able to hold his or her own, so that there is satisfaction all round.

JEERING

Pity the child who has no teeth in the front—he'll be taunted with:

> Gummy, gummy, goo,
> Half-past two,
> Put him in the letter-box
> And see what he'll do.
> I'm telling the nun
> You stole a bun,
> You put it in your pocket,
> And you gave me none.
> *or*
> Gummy, gummy, goo,
> Half-past two,
> Tuppence worth of starch,
> And a ha'penny worth of blue.

Pity, too, the child who has the misfortune to have his head shaved.
This used to be a very common sight due to scabby heads and
ring-worm, but it is much more rare nowadays. It is no fun to be
called *baldy-sconce, baldy-conscience, baldy-nopper, baldy-peelo,*
or to be asked facetiously *What does baldy mean?* or to hear someone
say:

> He's baldy from boxing,
> And gummy from eating oatmeal.

The child wearing glasses is called *speckey four-eyes* and the tall
skinny girl is called *skinnymalink melodeon legs.*

The child seen with sugar on his bread will be called:

> Sugar babby, sugar babby,[1]
> One, two, three,

or will have the following verse chanted out at him:

> X-Y-Z,
> Sugar on your bread,
> Go to the Doctor
> Before you're dead.
>   *or*
> X-Y-Z,
> Sugar on your bread,
> Porridge in the morning
> And cocoa going to bed.

The coward or the faint-harted may run away, but it will be with:

> Cowardy, Cowardy, Custard,
> Dip your head in mustard,

ringing in his ears. The child who tells tales is called:

> Tell-tale tattler
> Buy a penny rattler.

This habit of jeering people is not confined to acquaintances. A
stranger passing by won't go unnoticed, you'll hear them call out:

---

[1] *abb* as in *abbey.*

15

ALL IN! ALL IN!

Ey—does your mother know you're out?
Missus, it's all in your hat!

A man wearing a conspicuous cap will be called:

Cap of apples!
or
Tuppence worth of cap
And three ha'pence worth of peak.

The man who looks in need of a hair cut will be called:

Starve the barber!

While waiting to see a bride they chant:

Here comes the bride,
Bandy and cockeyed.

A child called Paddy must get used to hearing:

Paddy whack,
Let a crack,
On the Lord Mayor's back.

Consequently *Whacker* is a very common nickname for anyone called Paddy. You will also notice this custom of adding *-er, -ier* and *-ser* to words wherever it is possible. Names like Mick, Paddy or Jem will invariably become *Mickser, Padser, Jemser*. The boy with red hair becomes *Redser*, or if his surname is Byrne or Smith he'll be called *Burr'ner* or *Smither*. The North Circular Road is shortened to *Norrier*, and even the Christian Brothers of North Brunswick Street School have accepted the school's local name *The Brunner*. To young and old Croke Park and Dalymount Park are known as *Croker* and *Dalyier*. Jackstones are called *Jackers*, and a steel marble is called a *steeler*. Likewise the fish and chip shop is the *chipper*. If you heard two boys rejoicing at having no *ecker* to do during the *holliers*, it's just that they have no exercise (home work) to do during the holidays.

Parodying surnames is a very common practice, and always follows the same pattern. It's done more in fun than with malice. Names like Doyle, Kelly, and Moore go like this:

16

Doyle, the boil,
The rick stick stoil.

—◆—

Kelly, the belly,
The rick stick stelly.

—◆—

Moore, the boor, (*or* the hoor),
The rick stick stoor.

Of course the jeerer doesn't get away without a reminder of the dire consequences of his jeering:

Sticks and stones
May break my bones,
But names will never hurt me.
When you're dead
And in your grave,
You'll pay for what you called me.
or
When I die
I'll lie in my grave,
And suffer what you called me.
You called me this,
You called me that,
You called me a big fat pussy-cat.

THE CHANCE TO CHANT

If you stare at a child inquisitively you'll be asked tartly:

What are you looking at? *or* What do you think you're looking at?

You might think you were smart and reply *Not much!* but you'll get back:

Look in the mirror and you'll see less!

Far better if you could chant as they would if the positions were reversed:

I'm looking at you,
Your eyes are blue,
Your face is like a kangaroo.

17

If your curiosity outsteps the bonds of friendship you'll be put nicely in your place with:

> Mind your own business,
> And don't mind mine.
> Kiss your own sweetheart
> And don't kiss mine.

You might be asked deliberately to look up at the sky or to look behind you in order to give them a chance to sing out:

> I made you look,
> I made you stare,
> I made the barber
> Cut your hair.
> He cut it long,
> He cut it short,
> He cut it with
> A knife and fork.

The chance to chant out a verse is never lost. The Corporation lamplighter, now regretably gone from the street-scene, was well used to the lines:

> Billy with the lamp,
> Billy with the light,
> Billy with the sweetheart
> Out all night.

A soldier who has the appearance of being a new recruit has to get used to the verse:

> You're in the army now,
> You're not behind the plough.
> You'll never get rich,
> Digging a ditch,
> You're in the army now.

A customary form of greeting among grown-ups is *Good morrow and good luck*, to which the children usually add laughingly *Says the crow to the duck*.

The child who gives something and then wants to take it back is reminded:

> Give a thing,
> Take it back,
> God will ask you
> Where is that.
> If you say you don't know,
> God will send you down below.

If a child belches or breaks wind without excusing herself, even her mother will admonish her:

> Beg your pardon
> In God's (holy) garden.

Others will laugh it off with:

> Where e'er you be
> let your wind go free.

If you happened to be caught out on April Fool's day you could redeem yourself, if it's after mid-day, with the lines:

> April Fool is gone past,
> You are a big jackass.
> *or*
> April Fool is dead and gone,
> You're the fool to carry it on.
> *or*
> Two potatoes in a pot,
> You're a fool and I'm not.

At the end of a day's play when each child goes off to her own house, one will say *Good night!* and another will instantly add:

> Good night, sleep tight,
> Don't let the bugs bite.

Many of these children may never have actually seen a bug or realise that perhaps it was because of the *buggy* state of the tenement room in which they lived that their parents got the house they now occupy in the suburbs. But very few can escape hearing the word because it's in common use in reference to most old tenement houses.

Indeed, bugs and tenement rooms are almost synonymous. At one time the rent of a room was determined by the extent of the bugs. These bugs are small, oval-shaped, many-legged, and of a reddish colour. They breed very freely anywhere in an old house, even in the iron of a bed—hence the line·

> Don't let the bugs bite.

But the best breeding-ground is provided by the layer upon layer of wallpaper on old and poor walls. They breed so quickly it's almost impossible to get rid of them once they get in. My father believed that it was the actual composition of the walls which encouraged the bugs. It is believed that cow- or horse-hair was mixed with the plaster to give it a grip and bind it, and as the houses decayed it was this hair that caused the bugs to breed.

You don't need to have a very sharp nose to tell if a room is *buggy* the instant you set foot in it. And there are as many opinions on what a *buggy* smell is as there are bugs. My grandmother always said that they had the same smell as well-washed and dried clothes just brought in from the fresh air. This does seem contradictory but may be explained by the fact that many of the people living in these old tenement rooms have a reputation for almost fanatical cleanliness and are constantly waging war on the bugs with various solutions and mixtures that help to curb them and keep a fresh smell in the rooms. But whatever the explanation, bugs will remain in the everyday speech of Dublin as long as the tenements themselves remain.

RITUAL

The word 'ritual' is very often on the lips of adults when talking about certain habits or customs—*that was the ritual with them on a Saturday night* (that's what they always did on . . .), *that was their ritual of a (at) Christmas* (their custom). Children don't use the word 'ritual' but in fact many quite simple things are done with an unconscious sense of ritual.

SPIN, SPOUT, OR . . .

When the boys have a row it usually culminates in a boxing match and ends almost as soon as it began. But with the girls it's a much more subtle and complicated affair. Little girls who have quarrelled and consequently are 'not speaking' say they are *black out* with each other. Sides are taken by all the other pals so that a state of feud develops with copious tale-bearing and back-biting. During this time when one of the opposite side passes, they cough haughtily and say:

Ahem! to the dirt.

But this state of affairs doesn't last very long. A peace-maker is found and she brings about a reconciliation in an approved manner. After hearing the two sides of the row she ascertains which side is prepared to allow her to make friendly overtures on its behalf to the other side. She then approaches the child originally involved and asks on behalf of her opposite number:

(*Name*) says are you spin spout or black out.

Just for perversity she may say she is still *black out* but eventually after much coming and going she will declare herself *spin spout* and so the breach is healed, and friendship flourishes stronger than ever—until the next row starts.

RAIN, RAIN, COME DOWN

When it's threatening rain you'll hear:

Rain, rain, come down,
I owe you half a crown.
Rain, rain, go up,
I owe you half a cup.

PIE, PIE, COME OUT

When children fill toy buckets with sand at the sea-side or with clay in their own gardens, there is then the little ritual of charming *the pie* to come out. The bucket is turned upside down, then left like this while they start beating it with a little wooden spade, or a piece of wood, or just the hand, all the time chanting:

Pie, pie, come out,
I owe you half a clout.

After repeating this several times the bucket is raised, very gingerly, to reveal *the pie*.

SHUT YOUR EYES

A child may be so generous that you could truthfully say of her:

> She'd give you the bit out of her mouth,

and this is literally what she would do with no regard on either side for the laws of hygiene. But first she'd ask the favoured one to:

> Shut your eyes,
> And open your mouth,
> And see what God will send you.

CURTNESS

Yet children can be brief and to the point when it suits them, like saying to someone eating an apple *Butts on you!* instead of the long-drawn-out *Leave me the butt of the apple you're eating.* They have words at will when it comes to making a curt reply. Some replies don't even make sense, while others are the essence of logic.

> *She* did it
> Who's *she?*
> The cat's mother!

Someone accused of something, or asked to account for some deed, may just answer defensively—*Well!* But this meagre reply won't do at all, she'll be told with alacrity *A well is a place for water.* It is completely acceptable to shut someone up with such a phrase. But there are times when discretion prevails and silence is golden. That is, when a child states emphatically *My mother said . . .* or *My mother told me . . .* She is never doubted openly by her pals because they know if she was, they'd be asked crisply *Were you born before my mother?* and no self-respecting child would allow herself to be left speechless by such a question.

SUPERSTITIONS

Children have their superstitions too. If an ambulance approaches at any time they hold their collars while it is passing, to ensure that the person inside won't die.

SEE A PIN

A pin is always picked up with the accompanying verse as an explanation:

> See a pin,
> Pick it up,
> All the day
> You'll have good luck.
> See a pin,
> Pass it by,
> You'll want a pin
> Before you die.

MY STRAW BAMER

When men wore straw bamers[1] in the summer, children used to try to count a hundred of them and so get their wish. The first to catch sight of one claimed it with the words:

> My straw bamer one, two, three,
> Nobody has one only me.

THE BANSHEE

The banshee (Irish: *bean si,* fairy woman) is said to 'follow' certain families. That is to say, she may be heard crying (or wailing) during the night portending the death of a member of such a family. She may be heard by the family in question and (or) by neighbours (whom she also 'follows') who recognise the eerie sound and expect to hear of a death the next day. On being wakened by the cry of the banshee at night one always prays for a departing soul, whoever it may be. The banshee is imagined as a woman distraught with grief combing her long silky hair as she cries in the night. She is never heard in the day, but a comb seen on the ground, especially in the morning, is never touched because it is believed to belong to the banshee. If you touched that comb she would be sure to haunt you. A child who is constantly crying for no apparent reason is often said to be *crying someone out of the house.* The reference here is to the banshee.

---

[1] A man's straw hat is called a bamer in parts of Dublin. Originally applied only to the boater.

23

Pure Devilment

A RUN-AWAY KNOCK

The amusements and delights of the children are as numerous and varied as the children themselves. Some of these amusements are pure devilment, like knocking on a neighbour's door and running away, tying a long length of thread to a neighbour's door-knocker at night, and harassing the poor man by knocking from a safe hiding-place until the thread is discovered. Some people are smart enough to recognise a run-away knock and they don't answer it, much to the disgust of the culprits. Then they may run off to the newsagents and knock down the placards outside, then run away hoping the owner may chase them even a short distance.

BOXING THE FOX

In the autumn no apple tree in any garden is safe from the boys. Nothing gives them greater pleasure than the challenge of an apple tree laden with fruit, and the chance to *box the fox* (rob the orchard). When done successfully, it makes any boy the envy of all his pals and the favourite with the girls who get share of the spoils. But his pleasure in this popularity may be short-lived, for when he comes within sight of his own house who can blame him if he quails a little at his sister's exaggerated forebodings: *Just wait till you're got in! You're going to be creased! killed! massacred!*

7. They will always prefer the thrills and excitement of swinging on a lamp-post (p. 25)

8. Performing all sorts of acrobatic feats like the *duck* (p. 25)

9. Swinging in a different setting

10. In the shadow of the Black Church

SCUTTING

Another delight is the practice of *scutting* behind a car. That is, getting a jaunt or a *scut* or, as the boys say, a *goffo* on the back bumper of a car, unknown to the driver, or in the case of a lorry or van, gripping any hand-hold available and hanging on as long as possible—usually until some onlooker attracts the driver's attention by calling *Scut the whip!* or *Scut behind the car!* Little boys love to boast about the great scut they got after the milk-car or the laundry-van, the best scut of all being provided by the bin-men's car, because of the rail across the back, and of course there's the extra satisfaction of having outwitted the bin-men who are very vigilant for those who *scut behind the car.*

SWINGING ON A LAMP-POST

No matter what conventional playgrounds are provided for children to keep them off the streets they will always prefer the thrills and excitement of swinging on a lamp-post and performing all sorts of acrobatic feats like *the duck* and *the wild man* to the more sedate pleasures of the playground merry-go-round. To make a swing on a lamp-post you need a long length of rope. The two ends are tied together with a firm knot, then secured to the lamp-post at a height that will leave the 'seat' of the swing the right distance from the ground. This is determined by the height of the child who, when seated, should be able to use her feet comfortably against the base of the lamp-post for impetus, if there isn't another child standing by to give her a shove off. To prevent the rope from slipping, the lamp-post is moistened with spit before securing the rope. A coat or a cardigan folded up makes the 'seat' more comfortable. Two or three children can have a swing from the lamp-post at the same time. The *duck* and the *wild man* are performed for variety and daring. The *duck* means *ducking* or turning under, when you have swung far enough out that you don't knock your head off the lamp-post as you *duck*. The *wild man* is more difficult. For this you part the rope wide enough to allow your head through, then with a hand on each rope you keep turning around as you swing. Swinging on a lamp-post can be very dangerous which may account for its excitement and popularity. The first swing on a lamp-post usually appears around the middle of February. Like most street-games the craze doesn't last very long, nor does a child spend much time actually swinging. The absorbing and satisfying thing for the child is the erecting of the swing. Since two or three children can have a swing from the lamp-post at the same time, there is the added pleasure of shared excitement while swinging.

Make-Believe

PLAYING HOUSE

However, the swing (on lamp-post or gate) will be hastily abandoned as soon as a few more children gather around and one suggests *Play House!* This is more a piece of make-believe than a game. It is played by girls and boys together. The girls are usually aged up to twelve or thirteen, and the boys up to six or seven. *Playing House* gives each child a chance to be as expressive as possible in every way. First of all, the various 'parts' are allotted or assumed (though not without dispute). It is usually agreed that the eldest girl should be the 'Mother'. Perhaps because the boys are so much younger, there is seldom if ever a 'Father' appointed. The next two or three girls allot themselves other family positions: *I must be the Auntie* says one; *No,* says another, *I must be the Auntie and you must be the Granny;* another will opt to be *an Auntie who has a daughter getting married.* The younger girls and all the boys are the 'Children'. The 'Children' are seated along the kerb which forms one wall of the 'House'. From this the outline of the rest of the 'House' is drawn on the ground with chalk. It can be as elaborate and imaginative as you please. If you want to extend a room here or there you just rub out the chalk line vigorously with the sole of your shoe and draw another one to suit you. Of course the 'Children' don't just sit meekly in a line—not at all—they try to enter each room as it takes shape and are kept in their places only by threats and promises from the 'Mother'. If things get out of hand she wields the cane, doling out slaps as the teacher might at school. But whereas they must submit at school, here they can resort to all sorts of tricks to avoid the cane—much to the enjoyment of the other 'Children' and to the feigned frustration of the 'Mother'. This make-believe can develop along any pattern you wish; it only requires someone to say *I must be the Granny who comes to visit all her grandchildren!* and a concert takes place. When 'Granny' comes to the door she makes the gesture of opening the door—then she says *Tick* to indicate that she has turned the handle. She greets all the children, and then the 'Mother' decides that each child must do something to entertain 'Granny'. Here the children can give full rein to their imaginations and any latent talent a child may have is brought forth. There is no coaxing them to perform because they are only too eager to show 'Granny', and indeed each other, how talented they are. One will sing and another will dance and maybe someone else will recite a poem. When 'Granny' departs the 'Mother' will commence the formidable task of getting the children to bed. No sooner has she got them all lying down and feigning sleep than one will 'wake up' and ask for a drink of water. While 'Mother' is gone to get the water another will decide to run around the room and when 'Mother' comes back she'll have to chase her to get her back to bed again. After a few minutes it's morning and there's the ritual of getting them off to school and at this point the game may merge into a game of 'School' with the 'Mother' taking on the role of 'Teacher'. There is no end to the variations of this game. As I have said, it only requires someone to say *I must be this* or *I must do this*—and the make-believe continues from one situation to another.

PLAYING MOTHERS

When there are only three or four children available they may decide to play 'Mothers'. In this case each child is a 'Mother' and each carries a 'Baby'. This can be a doll, or a square of blanket or a cardigan folded into a sort of triangle to look like a child wrapped in a shawl. One 'Mother' may have a pram for her baby, but others wanting one make do with an empty shoe-box with a string attached to draw it along. If each child can get old high-heeled shoes so much the better. Whereas *House* is played by both boys and girls, and concerns only one 'Mother' and her 'Children' and 'Relatives', 'Mothers' is a group of three or four little girls (usually not older than ten years) imitating their own mothers. In this piece of make-believe you notice how observant small children are of the mannerisms and speech of their mothers. Everything is copied, the 'Babies' are fed, settled and re-settled, hushed to sleep with comments to one another on how cross the 'Baby' is, due to teething or maybe thrush. Another may declare she has been walking the floor all night with her 'Baby' because it has the *hookin* (whooping) cough. It is very interesting and pleasant to watch little girls *Playing Mothers*. You see the absorbed faces as little hands take infinite care with every detail of making the 'Baby' comfortable. You hear no shrieks of laughter now, for being a 'Mother' is a serious business.

PLAYING SHOP

Playing Shop is always great fun. An upturned box, the door-step or the kerb-stone will do for the 'Premises'. Chanies are used for 'Money' and clay brought to the proper consistency with water is used for 'Butter'. The 'Butter' is very important and gives the greatest pleasure, because it's a very satisfying experience to make the 'Butter', then to wield the 'clappers' vigorously to shape it into pounds or half-pounds. The 'Weighing Scales' is simply a piece of strong wood balanced across a large flat stone or brick. Laurel leaves, if available, are ideal for 'Rashers' and the seed-heads of wild dock are gathered for 'Tea'. The 'Tea' is also very important because it affords further opportunity to revel in the joys of weighing and measuring. Another vital commodity is 'Sweets', and quite a realistic display is provided by gathering sweet-papers and wrapping small stones in them. Empty cigarette boxes and any other empty cartons available complete the shop. When all is ready the customers are attracted by the following verse chanted repeatedly:

Buy a-way buy away a new shop o-pen. Hams, jams, an--ything you want ma'm.

Buy away, buy away,

A new shop open.

Hams, jams, anything you want ma'm.

Simple Pleasures

The children are never at a loss for amusement, and it will be noted that conventional toys have no part in their activities. The simple objects used for some of the games cost nothing, yet they can become to a child what a tool is to a tradesman. An empty spool, odd pieces of wool, a length of twine, two empty tins, these are a challenge to the imagination and creative powers of a child.

STILTS

An ideal pair of stilts can be made with two empty tins (cocoa-tins are very suitable), and two lengths of strong twine. Children of all ages, both boys and girls enjoy these stilts. They are simplicity itself to make. First the lids are removed and the tins are turned base upwards. Then to make the first stilt, the child places his foot on one of the tins and marks a spot on the base, each side of his foot. He then pierces a small hole at each mark. These holes are usually made by driving a nail through with a stone. Next a length of twine is threaded through the holes and the two ends are brought up evenly together. The child then places his foot on the tin, and taking the ends of the twine in his hands, he stands up on the stilt. He then ties the two ends together at a point which enables him to hold the twine tautly so that he can keep his balance on the stilt (the joining knot should be the centre of the hand-hold).

The second stilt is made in the same way. Since the lids are removed there is a particular 'plonk-plonk' sound when the children are stamping along on these stilts. And since they are not very high they are quite safe even for a small child. If only one tin is available, or a child wishes to lend one to another child who has none, there is a lot of fun stamping along up and down on one stilt.

A PEEP-SHOW

An empty shoe-box is another great source of pleasure, because with it you can make *A Peep-Show*. You make small holes all over the lid with a large nail or a wooden meat-skewer. Into the holes you insert pieces of coloured paper. Transparent coloured sweet-papers are best. You get the effect of small coloured 'lights' by pressing the centre of each paper down through the hole with your little finger. The inside of the box is then decorated with whatever is available, cut-out pictures, 'scraps', silver or gold foil, etc. You then cut a square in the front of the box for looking through, replace the lid and call out repeatedly:

A pin to see the show!

and you can be sure someone else will add:

The lady on the po.

It's not that you earn many pins but there is a huge amount of satisfaction and enjoyment in making 'the show'.
The peep-show has lost much of its popularity in the past few years.

WORKING WITH WOOL

Using up odd lengths of wool by making multi-coloured crochet rugs is a very popular occupation with little girls during the summer. They sit in a row along the kerb, talking incessantly while diligently plying their needles. It is lovely to see four or five girls sitting thus, each with a multi-coloured rug, now large enough to spread over her knees, getting larger and more colourful as she continues to work on it.
Making long narrow cords is another way of using up odd lengths of wool. This regrettably, is no longer popular, due perhaps to the ever-increasing use of plastic and cardboard spools for thread.

For making these cords an ingenious little 'loom' was made by inserting four small tacks around the hole of an empty wooden spool to form a square. Next, four stitches were 'cast on' to the tacks (one on each tack) as you would for knitting, to form a basic row. Another row was made by simply winding the wool once around the tacks. Then with a short knitting-needle or even a long thin nail, each bottom stitch was slipped over the thread above it, leaving one row of stitches again on the tacks. Another row was made by winding the wool once around the tacks as before. Again each bottom stitch was slipped over the thread above it, and then again the wool was wound around the tacks as before, and again each basic stitch slipped over the thread above it. The stitches thus slipped, form a narrow seamless cord. As the cord begins to form, it is brought through the hole in the spool and becomes as long as the supply of wool will allow.

I can't remember ever using these cords for any particular purpose; but like most occupations of childhood, the important thing was the patient preparation of the 'loom' and the fascination of seeing the multi-coloured cord emerging, ever so slowly, from the hole in the spool.

JINNY-JOE'S EGGS

Catching *Jinny-Joe's Eggs* is another absorbing pleasure. A *Jinny-Joe* is what we call the thistle-down that comes floating in the air on a summer's evening. It's amazing how many of these you can see even if you can't catch them, if you stand on an open green facing the light summer breeze. If you catch one and there's 'an egg' (a seed) in it, you put the 'egg' in a matchbox. If there is no 'egg' in it then you blow it away from the palm of your hand saying:

Jinny-Joe, Jinny-Joe, lay me an egg.

CATCHING BEES

Grown-ups will always admonish children for the cruelty of catching bees in a jam-jar, and mutilating flowers and hedges in the process. They ask *How would you like to be put to suffocate in a jam-jar?* But children never give a moment's thought to such an unlikely event. They wait patiently and silently for *a bumbler* (a bumble-bee) to land on a flower or a hedge within reaching-distance of them. Then with practised skill they get the bee into the jar which is already crammed with flowers and other bees. This is done with the aid of a piece of cardboard used as a lid. If the bee lands too far away they often unconsciously risk life and limb reaching up to capture it, flower and all, into the jam-jar.

DO YOU LIKE BUTTER?

Children can tell if you like butter by holding a buttercup under your chin and if the yellow is reflected there—you like butter.

ONE O'CLOCK

The seed-head of the dandelion is usually called a 'one o'clock' because it's used to tell the time. You begin by blowing and saying *It's one o'clock*, and so on, until the whole 'clock' has been blown away. Whatever time reached at the end is declared the right time by the children who probably couldn't read the clock anyhow.

IT WILL, IT WON'T

Any question can be settled by picking off the petals of a daisy to the words:

> It will, it won't; it will, it won't (rain, etc.).
> You have, you haven't; you have, you haven't
> (a sweetheart, an uncle in America, etc.).

HELL, HEAVEN, PURGATORY OR LIMBO

Everything is a source of entertainment—even the buttons on a dress or cardigan. Children can't resist naming off the buttons on each others' clothes to ascertain 'where you will go when you die' *Hell, Heaven, Purgatory* or *Limbo*. These four places are repeated until all the buttons are counted. Whichever one you stop at, that's 'where you will go when you die'.

BADGES

Other sources of fun are the metal caps on bottles which can be made into badges. Just remove the cork lining from the cap and put it inside your dress, hold it in place and allow it to protrude a little. Then snap the metal cap over the protrusion and there, you have a badge.

COMB AND PAPER

Nothing is wasted. The tissue paper which lines the silver paper in a packet of cigarettes goes around a comb to make music, and the silver paper is kept to decorate a peep-show or a spinning-top.

A BUZZ

You'll often hear one child saying to another *Give us* (me) *a buzz*. This is done by each child catching the other's crossed hands and swinging round and round as fast as they can.

A LEG AND A DUCK

If you heard a young child saying to an older one *Give us* (me) *a leg and a duck*, and if the older one agreed, this is what you would see: The older child taking hold of the younger one by the right hand and the right ankle and swinging her round and round.

SHAKE THE BLANKET

Shake the blan--ket, shake the blan--ket, turn the blan--ket o--ver.

Shake the blanket,

Shake the blanket,

Turn the blanket—over.

You'll hear two children chanting this while they go through the actions of the verse. They face each other holding hands, then raise them up and down—shaking the blanket. At the words *turn the blanket—over* they each try to turn under the other's hands without letting go, but it usually ends in confusion.

CARRY A LADY TO LONDON

The same two may then try to *Carry a Lady to London*. For this they form a seat with their crossed hands and a third child takes the seat to be carried to London—but they seldom get very far.

JACK, JACK

All the children hop around on one foot repeatedly invoking an unknown and unseen Jack:

> Jack, Jack, keep me up the longest.

KING OF THE CASTLE

A child can mount a step or a small heap of stones and declare:

> I'm the king of the castle,
> Go down (*or* out) you dirty rascal.

and having made this claim he then endeavours to hold his position against all others who try to bring him down.

Dexterity

HOT HANDS

I suppose few games evoke such a concentrated effort as *Hot Hands*. When children get the craze for it they never seem to stop. They enjoy it just as much with an adult if they can't get another child to play it, or if they want to improve their technique—and indeed adults get quite a lot of fun out of it too.

Two children, boys or girls, sit or stand facing each other and while they chant the verse they perform the following actions with their hands.

1. Each girl claps her hands together once.
2. Each girl claps her hands to the two hands opposite her—that is, one girl's right hand claps the other girl's left hand and her left hand claps the other girl's right hand.
3. Each girl claps her hands together.
4. Each girl claps the right hand of the other girl.
5. Each girl claps her hands together.
6. Each girl claps the left hand of the other girl.
7. Each girl claps her hands together.

2, 3, 4, 5, 6, 7 are repeated again and again and the verse is chanted in tune with the movements and gets progressively faster each time. It usually ends in confusion and laughter.

The following are some of the verses used for *Hot Hands:*

DEXTERITY

Mrs. D — Mrs. I,
Mrs. F — F — I,
Mrs. C — Mrs. U,
Mrs. L — T — Y:
D I F F I C U L T Y .

—◆—

3, 6, 9,
The goose drank wine,
The monkey chewed tobacco
In the Streets of Caroline.
The line broke,
The monkey choked,
And they all went to heaven
In a little rowing boat.
Clap Clap.

—◆—

My Mammy sent me to the shops one day,
And told me what to say, say, say.
And there I met a pretty little boy,
Who offered me to stay, stay, stay.
He offered me some peaches,
He offered me some pears,
He offered me his twenty cents
To kiss him on the stairs, stairs, stairs.
I do not want your peaches,
I do not want your pears,
And I do not want your twenty cents
To kiss you on the stairs, stairs, stairs.

The following version is the same as the one above for the first
four lines then changes to:

Johnny gave me apples,
Johnny gave me pears,
Johnny gave me sixpence
To kiss him on the stairs.
I gave him back his apples,
I gave him back his pears,
I gave him back his sixpence,

And flung him down the stairs.
He jumped in the lake,
And he swallowed a snake,
And he came back up
With a belly-ache.

This verse is also used for skipping or hopping a ball, or playing ball against a wall.

CHESTNUTS

The Phoenix Park being only a stone's throw away from our neighbourhood, there is never any difficulty in having a good supply of chestnuts when the autumn comes around for a game of *chessers*. A narrow hole is bored through the fresh chestnut (it would be very difficult to bore a hole through a chestnut which has become seasoned). A knot is made in the end of a length of twine, and the twine is threaded through the hole. Then the idea is to smash the greatest number of other chestnuts with your own. To get first crack at your opponent you say as soon as you see him:
Hick, hack, first crack!
At this, he holds out his piece of twine on which he has a chestnut and you take a crack at it. If you manage to smash his chestnut your own chestnut is now called a *conker* (conqueror) of one. But if you smash your own, your opponent gets the credit of one. In fact the boys always call their chestnuts *conkers*! If a boy is smart he can keep a good big chestnut until the next year when it becomes a *seasoner* and therefore so hard it can be truly said to be a *conker of fifty* or more. Girls don't play chestnuts, but the boys never hesitate to boast to them about how many they have conquered, and the girls are always suitably impressed.

MOWL

Another game played almost exclusively by the boys is *Mowl* (*-owl* as in *howl*). This is played by lifting open the small cover of the water hydrant and aiming small flat stones or if possible, coins (two new pence) into it. The distance from which to shoot is agreed upon and they line up for their chance. A player may land his coin directly into the mowl or within *spanners*—a distance that can be spanned with the tip of his outstretched thumb and the tip of his middle finger. Then he can stand on the water hydrant

38

and aim at the coin of another player. If he strikes it he can claim that coin, or if money is scarce he can just chalk up five points for himself. The length of time the boys spend playing this game and the amount of concentration spent on each throw is amazing.

FIVE SLATES

I haven't seen *Five Slates* played this long time, but it used to be very popular with the girls in summer.

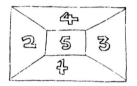

For this simple but absorbing street-game each child had her own five pieces of slate or five small flat stones. A reasonable throwing distance was agreed upon, and a line drawn. Each aimed at getting as high a score as possible. If the slate or stone touched a line you scored nothing. Each child's name was written on the ground and her total score in each round chalked down to her.

JACKSTONES

Boys and girls used to play *Jackstones* with equal enthusiasm and dexterity. It is seldom played nowadays and only by the boys. Anyone who has ever played *Jackstones* will understand what it meant to a child to acquire five well-shaped jackstones. Anyone who hasn't, may find it hard to believe that five little stones could become to a child a very precious possession. You don't get the five stones together right away. The first five stones enable you to carry on with the game, but one by one you discard them in favour of stones you have decided are the ideal ones for you—that is, ones which are the right size and shape. This may take some time. The more rounded they are the easier they are to pick up from the ground during play, yet if they are too round they are liable to roll too far away and this is a nuisance. So, having found the right five you have the feeling of having five special friends. They

39

are carried everywhere, and it is always re-assuring to feel the familiar little shapes in your pocket when you're in the bad books at home or relations with other pals are strained. That is one of the great advantages of *Jackstones,* you can become completely absorbed in the various movements even by yourself. Indeed every opportunity to improve your game is availed of, so that you can show your skill to the next child who comes along offering to give you a game of *Jackers.* The doorstep or the kerb are the most popular places for settling down to a game of *Jackstones.* Each game consists of various rounds, each of which must be performed without a mistake before you win a game. If you fail at a round you must wait until your turn comes again. When referring to the various rounds you say—in the case of Game 1—*I'm for two's* or *I'm for three's,* whatever the round may be. In the case of Game 2 you say *I'm for two-a-bar* or *I'm for three-a-bar. Jackstones* are played with one hand only.

Game 1

First Round

Have the five stones in the palm of your hand. Throw them all together in the air and catch one of them descending on the back of your hand. If you catch more than one, or none at all, you are 'out' and it is the turn of the next child. When your turn comes again you try once more and when you get one on the back of your hand, you throw it again in the air (from the back of your hand) and catch it in your hand.

Second Round

The same as above, but this time you must catch *two* stones on the back of your hand (any other number and you are 'out', as before). When you get the two on the back of your hand you throw them up and catch them in your hand.

Third Round

This time you must get three on the back of your hand, and then four, and finally (usually after many failures), you get five on the back of your hand. When you have succeeded in throwing up these five stones and catching them again all together you have completed this game.

11. Getting a shove off (p. 25)

12. Hopping on one foot she kicks the pickey from bed to bed never letting down the other foot

13. The number of boys to be seen playing beds has increased considerably (p. 153)

14. An empty shoe-polish or ointment tin makes an ideal pickey (p. 153)

Game 2

First Round

Toss the five stones out in front of you. Pick out one and toss it in the air. Before you catch it again pick up one of the four stones on the ground. Then, in the same hand, catch the descending stone. Put one of the stones aside. Toss the stone in your hand in the air, and before you catch it again, pick up one of the remaining three stones. Repeat as before until you have set all the stones aside.

Second Round

Toss the five stones out in front of you as before. Pick out one stone and toss it in the air. Before you catch it again, pick up two stones. then catch the descending one. Put two of these stones aside and toss the other one in the air. Pick up the two remaining stones from the ground, then catch the descending one. In this round, you must be careful after you toss the five stones out in front of you, to select the one for tossing up that will leave the remaining four in the best position to be taken in twos.

Third Round

Toss the five stones out in front of you. Pick out one stone and toss it in the air. Before you catch it again, pick up one of the four stones on the ground. Then catch the descending one and put one of these aside. Now toss the other one in the air and pick up the three remaining stones from the ground before you catch the descending one. Here again you must be careful to select the stone for tossing up and the one stone you pick up so that the three stones remaining on the ground are best placed for picking up together.

Fourth Round

When you have tossed out the five stones in front of you, select one stone and toss it in the air. Then pick up the remaining four all together before you catch the descending one. Again select the stone for tossing up that will leave the remaining four in the best position to be picked up all together.

Those four rounds complete that game.

Game 3

Toss all five stones in the air. Catch one on the back of your hand. Toss this in the air (from the back of your hand) and before you catch it again in your hand, pick up one of the four stones from the ground. Leave one of these aside. Now toss four stones in the air and catch one on the back of your hand. Toss it up as before and pick up one of the three stones on the ground. Repeat as above until all the stones have been laid aside.

Having completed these three games you can now go on to the following feats of dexterity called *Cracks*, *No Cracks*, *Clutch*, *Fingies*, and finally *Home*.

Cracks

Toss the five stones in the air. Whatever number lands on the back of your hand, toss them up again and catch them in your hand in such a way that they hit off each other. This hit is called a *crack*. If you have two in your hand at this stage, leave one aside (if you have three, leave two aside) and toss the remaining one in the air. Then pick up one of the three from the ground, and catch the descending one with a *crack*. Repeat until you have taken all the stones with a *crack*.

No Cracks

This is done the same way as *Cracks* except that this time the stones must not hit off each other. This is very difficult at the beginning if more than two stones land on the back of your hand. Two is the ideal number, because you can catch one in your palm and the other between your thumb and forefinger. More than two and it is very difficult to catch them together with *no cracks*.

Clutch

Toss up the five stones. Whatever number lands on the back of your hand toss these up again and catch them in your hand. If you have three in your hand, keep (or *clutch*) two in your closed fist and throw up the third one with your thumb and forefinger. Before you catch it again, you must pick up one of the two remaining on the ground. Now keep three in your closed fist and throw up the fourth. Before you catch it again pick up the fifth one from the ground.

Fingies

Toss up the five stones and whatever number lands on the back of your hand leave there. Now, without letting these fall, open your fingers and catch the stones remaining on the ground between your fingers. Then toss up the ones on the back of your hand and catch them in your palm, at the same time get the one's between your fingers into your palm without letting any of them fall.

Home (*This is the house that Jack built*)

Place four stones in a square like this:

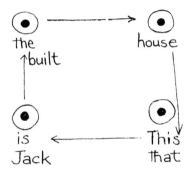

Begin at the lower right corner, and with the fifth stone in your hand, touch each stone in the square with a word saying: *This is the house that Jack built*. This takes you to the top left corner. At the word *built* toss up the stone in your hand and before catching it again pick up the other stone.
Leave this stone aside.

Next start at the lower left corner and repeat *This is the house that Jack built*. This takes you to the top right corner, where you toss up the stone in your hand, and before catching it again pick up the other stone. Leave this stone aside. Begin the next round at the top left corner, and you will demolish the lower right corner. Finally, begin at the top right corner and you will demolish the last corner, the lower left. You have now completely demolished *the house that Jack built* so you must now go through the ritual of re-building it. This is how you do it:

Toss the five stones out in front of you. Select one of them (one that will leave the other four in the best position to be taken one at a time). Now with this stone, describe the proposed square. Begin at the bottom right corner as illustrated above.

Hit the top left hand corner which you reach at *built,* toss the stone in the air, and pick up one of the four stones before you catch it again. Place one of these stones in this corner. Begin the next round at the bottom left corner and repeat the first movement and you will replace the top right corner-stone. Continue until you have replaced the four stones and re-built the house. To end the session of *Jack-stones* you demolish the house again by tossing one stone in the air, and picking up the four corner-stones of Jack's house all together, before catching it again. You can now deposit the five little stones in the familiar confines of your pocket to take a well-earned rest until the next session.

SPINNING A TOP

I know you could just buy a top and a lash and proceed to use them. But Dublin children would seldom do anything so straightforward and lacking in ceremony. It would seem that in order to compensate for having to buy the top, an elaborate amount of preparation must go into the decoration of it, and also into the making of the lash.

There is a common belief in Dublin that chalk creates sickness. This of course may be just a ruse by grown-ups to try and discourage the use of chalk. For it must be admitted that once there is chalk to be had, either from old plaster or someone's opulence in being able to buy a box of coloured chalk, no surface escapes. 'Beds' are chalked and re-chalked on every available inch of ground and walls are covered with slogans, and mottos and various drawings.

Before a top is set spinning the flat surface is always decorated with a design done in coloured chalk(s). Any previous design is rubbed off with a spit, dried, and re-done with a different design. These efforts at design may be the first and last attempts at artistic self-expression that these children ever experience, or they may lead to greater artistic development. The scope for design on such a small surface is very limited, but this very limitation is in itself a challenge to the imagination and ingenuity of the child. The designs are of necessity very simple and are usually geometrical. But it is the colours used that produce the full effect when the top is spinning. So, it must always be remembered that no matter how pretty a top looks in the hand, the aim is to create a design suitable to the high speed of the top when it is spinning. Rivalry is very keen, and the individual touches used to obtain special effects when the top is spinning can be the envy of all. Some of these touches may be no more than a speck or two of silver paper stuck on with a spit, or a tiny dab of a spit-moistened finger here and there on the well-chalked surface.

Next comes the preparation of the lash. Here again you could buy one in the shop, and many do, but it is never used as it is bought, because the lash part is usually a single length of leather thonging and absolutely useless for lashing a top, being always too long, too rigid, and generally tending to prevent the top spinning properly. The stick part is what you pay for, because this will be the right length, smooth to handle, and grooved or holed at the top to take the lash. So, if you buy one, you remove the thonging and replace it with your own strong twine. The best lash is made with double strands of twine or fine cord, the ends untwisted for a more even 'lash'.

If you must make your own, you get a piece of wood the proper length and smooth away the splinters as best you can. We were one time very fortunate in having the coffin-makers in the neighbourhood so that a good supply of the right wood was always assured. Lengths of waste moulding could be had for nothing and made an ideal stick. Next, a groove or notches is made in the top of the stick to hold the twine fast. If you cannot manage this, or a hole, a good spit around the stick and on the twine will ensure that it does not slip. A good lash is like a good pickey. You get used to the feel of it and you hate to have to lend it to anybody else. It will last you the whole season if properly cared for, requiring only a renewal of the twine. It is surprising how quickly the twine wears away when you are expert at lashing. Now you are ready to spin your top and you can please yourself about this too. You can take the top between the fingers of both hands and bending close to the ground, spin it. Or, you might be very skilled and use only the thumb and first finger of one hand. You could also hold the top aloft between both hands and spin it in mid-air first and see if it will remain spinning when it hits the ground. A little more ritualistic is the method of winding the twine, end first, around the groove at the top of the top. Then, holding the stick in your right hand and the top in your left, with a short length of the twine held very rigid in between, you swiftly let the lash loose and your delight should know no bounds when you find the top spinning away merrily. When the top is spinning at full speed you have lashed it into a *heat*. It will seem to be almost motionless, so swiftly is it spinning. At this speed you could bend close to it and having spit on your middle finger you gently touch the fast-spinning top and thereby change the design without stopping it.

If you have not got an ordinary top, the hard black screw-type of cork used in some mineral bottles will do, and being so small and light you can lash it a greater distance at a time. But if you cannot get even this, then you may be allowed to share someone else's top. For this you stand some distance away on the opposite side from the other child and when she lashes the top down in your direction you then lash it back to her. This can be even more fun than lashing a top on your own.

Unfortunately wooden spinning tops are becoming more and more scarce and so the sight of children lashing tops is becoming equally rare. If the children could make the tops themselves, this would never happen.

ROLLING YOUR HOOP

Mol - ly. I'd love to be rolling your hoop. rolling your hoop. rolling your hoop.

Mol - ly. I'd love to be rolling your hoop down by the counte - ry gar -- dens.

> Molly I'd love to be rolling your hoop,
>
> Rolling your hoop, rolling your hoop.
>
> Molly I'd love to be rolling your hoop,
>
> Down by the country gardens.

I passed the Corporation flats in Dorset Street recently and I noticed the modern playground included in the general lay-out. Some little girls were savouring the 'thrills' of the shining steel slide while others enjoyed the sand-pit. But a group of boys were gathered together away from the playground getting ready to roll their hoops around the block. No car-rally drivers could have been more intent on their preparations than these. Yes, the hoop is as popular as ever. In The Park they are heard rolling noisily about mid July every year. The craze does not last very long but it is quite intense while it does.

It is amazing how, quite suddenly, a fleet of hoops seems readily available.

A hoop is simply the discarded wheel of a bicycle minus the tyre and tube. Once it has been acquired as a hoop it is never again referred to as a wheel. A small piece of stick is used to roll it along and an odd tap on either side will keep it on a straight course or guide it around a bend. A hoop may be seen 'parked' against a railing or wall with this little stick balanced on top resting in the groove. The tops of the spokes which protrude into the groove afford an excellent means of 'braking'. All that is required to bring the hoop to a sudden halt is to put the top of the stick down into the groove and it gets a grip against these protrusions and the hoop stops dead still without toppling over.

Picking Sides

Picking sides or 'Man' for a game is no haphazard affair, it is usually decided by rhyme. The children (boys and girls) stand in a row and whichever child has suggested the particular game stands facing them and recites any one of a number of possible rhymes. She points to each child in turn including herself with every word.

> My mother and your mother
> Were hanging out the clothes.
> My mother gave your mother
> A punch on the nose.
> What colour was her blood?

The child pointed to at this last word mentions some colour: Yellow! which is then spelled out, each child getting a letter:

> Y-E-L-L-O-W spells yellow.

The child reached at the last word is 'on it' or it can be extended further with the additional line:

> And have you got this colour on you?

If she has the colour she is 'on it' or she is set free according to the game in question.

Other rhymes used for this purpose are:

> Amen means 'so be it'
> A half a loaf, a threepenny bit.
> Two men with four feet,
> Walking down O'Connell Street,
> Calling out 'Pigs feet,
> One and four a pound'.

—◆—

> Each a peach, a pear, a plum,
> Who is your very best chum?
> (The child reached at the last word mentions the
> name of her best chum)
> Eileen! (which is then spelled out, each child
> getting a letter)
> E-I-L-E-E-N spells Eileen.

Whoever gets the last word is 'on it'.

—◆—

> Each a peach, a pear, a plum,
> When does your birthday come?
> *or*
> Eena, meena,
> Tippy,teena.
> A, baa, booshalom
> When does your birthday come?

The child reached at 'come' tells her birthday, say the 8th of October.
Then October is spelled out, each child getting a letter, then eight
is counted out, each child getting a number. Whoever is reached at
eight is 'on it'.

The following rymes are also used for picking sides:

49

ALL IN! ALL IN!

Eena, meena,
Tippy, teena.
A, baa, booshalom,
X, Y, number nine,
Out goes you.
Out goes one,
Out goes two,
Out goes the little girl
All dressed in blue.
Birds in the garden,
Fishes in the sea,
If you want to pick one,
Please pick me.

---◆---

A pig went into a public house
To get a pint of porter.
'Where's your money'?
'In my pocket'
'Where's your pocket'?
'I forgot it'
'Please walk straight out'!

---◆---

As I went up some Chin-ese steps, I met some Chinese peo - - ple.

This is the way they spoke to me: Issa bissa bonka, issa bissa bonka and out goes she.

As I went up some Chinese steps,
I met some Chinese people.
This is the way they spoke to me:
Issa bissa bonka, issa bissa bonka,
And out goes she.

Green, white, and yellow,
My mother got a fellow.
The fellow died,
My mother cried,
Green, white, and yellow.

When I was young
I had no sense,
I bought a fiddle
For eighteen pence.
The only tune
That I could play,
Was cut the loaf
And eat away.

51

Where are you going Bob,
Down the lane Bob,
For what Bob,
For rhu-bob.
Let's go Bob,
No Bob,
Why Bob,
Because you don't like rhu-bob.

—◆—

I think, I think,
I smell a stink.
I think, I think,
I do.
I think, I think,
I smell a stink.
I think it's off
of *You*.

—◆—

Ink a pink,
A bottle of ink.
A cork cut out,
And you stink.

If one of only two children has to be decided on, it is done by the simple method of one of them turning her back to the rest and spitting on one of her palms. Then closing both fists and crossing them one over the other, she holds them out giving the other child a choice. If she chooses the wet palm she is 'on it' or 'out' or whatever it is that has to be decided. If she chooses the dry palm the other child is 'on it' or 'out'. Before making her choice she may chant this invocation:

Hail Mary full of grace,
Put me on the lucky place.

Ball Games

A child can do many things with a ball. Simply hop it up and down, throw it up in the air and catch it, throw it against a wall and catch it, throw it to another child who must catch it and throw it back to her. The more ambitious can do the same thing but with two or three balls in play at the same time. But this sort of play is very dull and does not last long. So, various actions which require skill and dexterity are introduced with accompanying rhymes. Each child gets her chance, competition is keen as the games won by each are chalked up, and so the hours fly by. Perhaps because of their interest in football, the boys don't play these ball games.

HOPPING A BALL

The simple action of hopping a ball becomes a game when it is accompanied by a rhyme and various actions. When you have completed the rhyme the first time without mishap, you are then *for steadies,* which means you repeat the rhyme and hop the ball but keep your two feet together. If you move them at all you are 'out'. When you succeed in getting past *steadies* you are then *for right foot*. For this you again repeat the rhyme and hop the ball with your right foot raised from the ground. After this you are *for left foot*. For this you repeat the rhyme and hop the ball with your left foot raised from the ground. There are other variations as in *Charlie*

Chaplin went to France. In this the *heel, toe,* are suitably demonstrated and for *over you go* the right leg is raised over the ball as it hops.

The following rhymes are used for this type of ball game:

> One, two, three, four,
> Jinny at the cottage door.
> Eating plums off a plate,
> Five, six, seven, eight.

—◆—

> One, two, three, four,
> I bumped my nose against the door.
> The door fell in,
> And I fell out,
> O-U-T spells Out.

—◆—

> One, two, three, four, five, six, seven,
> All good children go to heaven.
> When they die their sins are forgiven,
> One, two, three, four, five, six, seven.

—◆—

> Charlie Chaplin went to France,
> To teach the ladies how to dance,
> And this is the way he taught them:
> Heel, toe, over you go,
> Heel, toe, over you go,
> Heel, toe, over you go,
> And that's the way he taught them.

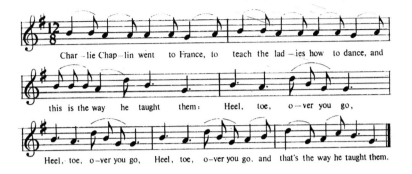

Char—lie Chap—lin went to France, to teach the lad—ies how to dance, and
this is the way he taught them: Heel, toe, o—ver you go,
Heel, toe, o—ver you go, Heel, toe, o—ver you go, and that's the way he taught them.

—◆—

Charlie Chaplin went to France,
To teach the ladies how to dance,
And this is the way he taught them:
Heel, toe, over we go,
All around the G.P.O.[1]

—◆—

My mother, my mother,
She married a black.
She went to the wedding
And never came back.
When she got back
She'd a hump on her back.
My mother, my mother,
She married a black.

—◆—

Little Nellie in her tent,
She can't afford to pay her rent.
The landlord came and put her out,
Put her out, put her out, put her out.
It's not because she's dirty,
It's not because she's clean,
But because she has the whooping-cough,
And the measles in between.

[1] General Post Office

55

ALL IN! ALL IN!

Lit-tle Nel-lie in her tent, she can't af-ford to pay her rent. The landlord came and put her out, put her out, put her out, put her out. It's not be-cause she's dir——ty, it's not because she's clean, but be-cause she has the whooping cough and the meas—les in be—tween.

Pounds, shillings and pence,
Mrs. Bates fell over the fence.
She fell so high,
She tipped the sky,
Pounds, shillings and pence.

Mary Anne,
Sat in the pan,
Forty years ago.

Mr. Flynn,
Broke his chin,
Sliding on
A banana skin.

In the following rhymes every time *O'Leary* is said the right leg is raised over the ball as it hops. The first three lines are spoken.

My Mammy said,
If she caught me playing with you,
She'd bring me upstairs and give me:

56

15. Donkey (p. 68)

16. Ready-made shop toys play no part in these street-games (p. 178)

17. Ring-a-ring-a-rosie (p. 12)
18. A-sha, a-sha, we all fall down (p. 12)

19. When you have no front gate swing from your Georgian doorway.

One. Two. Three. O' Leary. Four. Five. Six. O' Leary.

Sev – en. Eight. Nine. O' Leary. Ten. O' Leary. postman's knock.

1, 2, 3, O'Leary,
4, 5, 6, O'Leary,
7, 8, 9, O'Leary,
10, O'Leary,
Postman's knock.

Sometimes the first three lines of the above rhyme are omitted altogether or instead of the numbers the following words are used:

1, 2, 3, O'Leary,
I spy Miss O'Leary,
Sitting on her bum O'Leary
Eating chocolate soldiers.

———◇———

The inventiveness of the children in substituting new words to suit new environments is shown in the following version of the above rhyme. The main road to and from the Corporation housing estate in Finglas passes the Merville Dairies where ice-cream is made and where many of the tenants also work.

1, 2, 3, O'Leary,
I spy my Auntie Mary
Coming out of Merville Dairy,
Eating chocolate ice-cream.

———◇———

Gipsy, gipsy, Caroline,
Washed her hair in turpentine.
Turpentine makes it shine,
Gipsy, gipsy, Caroline.
('Queenie, queenie', is sometimes used instead of
'Gipsy, gipsy').

57

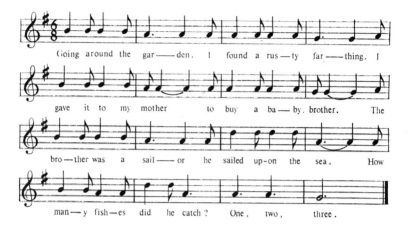

Going around the garden,
I found a rusty farthing.
I gave it to my mother,
To buy a baby brother.
The brother was a sailor,
He sailed upon the sea.
How many fishes did he catch?
One, two, three.

Long-legged Italy
Kicked poor Sicily
Into the middle
Of the Mediterranean Sea.
When Germany got Hungary
She eat a bit of Turkey,
Dipped it in Greece
And served it on China (*or* Japan).

Ashes to ashes,
Dust to dust.
If God won't have you,
The Devil must.

No one can come out of Hell,
For out of Hell there's no redemption.
When you get there you get your pension,
Tuppence a week for working hard,
Chasing the Devil around the yard.

—◇—

No one can come out of Hell,
For out of Hell there's no redemption.
When you get there you get your pension,
Tuppence a week and nothing more,
For chasing the Devil around the floor.

—◇—

One, two, three,
My mother caught a flea.
She put it in the teapot,
To make a cup of tea.
The flea jumped out,
My mother let a shout,
And in came my father
With his shirt hanging out.

—◇—

Billy the barber,
Shaved his father,
With a rusty razor.
The razor slipped,
And cut his lip,
Three cheers for Billy the barber.

—◇—

Baby's eyes are Irish,
Baby's eyes are blue,
Baby's eyes are Daddy's,
He was Irish too.
Daddy's gone to Heaven,
Gone to Paradise,
Leaving his little baby,
With two lovely Irish eyes.

Although 'Mark's Penny Bazaar' is remembered now by only the older generation, the memory of it lives on in the following rhyme. In this once famous bazaar everything cost a penny. It was situated at the top of Henry Street on the right-hand side going down from O'Connell Street. It was destroyed during the Easter Rising of 1916.

> Ma, let's go,
> To see the Rodeo.
> The Rodeo is not far,
> It's just beside the Penny Bazaar.
> The Penny Bazaar is not far,
> Ma, let's go!

I hope that version will continue for a long time yet, but recently I heard the following version which would seem to indicate a change, and indeed this is not surprising since the word bazaar is not in common use these days:

> Ma, let's go,
> To see the Rodeo.
> The Rodeo is not far,
> It's just behind the horse and car.
> The horse and car is not far,
> Ma, let's go—No!

See pp. 67, 149 for additional rhymes used for hopping a ball.

PLAYING BALL AGAINST A WALL

Wherever you have a smooth piece of wall or a flat door you'll find at least two girls each taking her turn at playing the ball against the flat surface. They may play with one ball only, but often they keep two or three balls going like a juggler. The actions are the important thing in these ball games, not the rhymes, which in some cases are hardly rhymes at all, but just a few almost meaningless words strung together like:

> Maypole butter, maypole tea,
> M-A-Y-P-O-L-E.

Maypole is spelled out so that the last E rhymes with tea. This derives from a chain of grocery shops called 'The Maypole'.

Another example of this use of simple everyday words is *Plainy packet of Rinso*. But as I have said, it's the actions accompanying the words that are important and which require an amount of skill and dexterity. So where you hear words like:

Plainy: The ball is simply thrown against the wall and caught.

Over: The ball is thrown against the wall in an over-arm action.

Downy: The ball is thrown against the wall then allowed to hop once off the ground before being caught.

Dashy: The ball is first hopped off the ground before it hits the wall and is then caught.

Right leg: As above except that the ball is hopped from under the right leg which is raised off the ground.

Left leg: The same as *Dashy* except that the ball is hopped from under the left leg which is raised off the ground.

Archy: The two feet are parted to form an 'arch' and the ball is hopped from behind, under the 'arch', to hop off the ground before it hits the wall and is then caught.

Backy: You turn sideways to the wall and hop the ball behind your back off the ground and onto the wall.

These are the most usual actions which accompany the rhymes. There are many more of course as I describe in *Plainy Clappy* and *I've a Bike*. Note that in this last one *Dashy, Downy,* and *Archy* become:

> I went up the hill,
> Down the hill,
> Under the arch,

to suit the action of the verse.

PLAINY CLAPPY

Plainy here simply means a plain throwing of the ball against the wall with no accompanying actions. But very often you will hear *clainy* or *claimy* instead, to alliterate with *clappy*.

> Plainy, clappy, rolley, to-backy,
> Hippy, tippy, a jelly-bag and a basket.

The words of this verse would be completely meaningless were it not for the actions which they denote.

Plainy: The ball is thrown against the wall and caught.
Clappy: The hands are clapped while the ball is in flight.
Rolley: The arms are 'rolled' one over the other.
To-backy: The hands are clapped behind the back.
Hippy: The hands are placed on the hips before catching the ball.
Tippy: The ground is tipped while the ball is in flight.
A jelly-bag: The two hands are placed together with the fingers apart and the ball is caught in this 'bag'.
A basket: The fingers of both hands are locked together and then with the knuckles towards you, the ball is caught in the locked palms or 'basket'.

If you get through this without dropping the ball you are then *for steadies.* For this you must go through the same thing again keeping your two feet together and not moving them during play. After that you're *for right foot.* For this you go through the formula again but with the right foot raised off the ground. Then you do it with the left foot raised off the ground and lastly you do it while your feet go through the motions of a step-dance (usually a reel). If you make a mistake during play the child next to you gets her chance and then the next, depending on how many are playing. When your turn comes round again you resume where you left off until you complete a game.

I'VE A BIKE

A little girl's two-wheel bicycle is usually called a 'fairy-bike'. During my childhood a fairy-bike was something only a fairy godmother could possibly bring you, being far beyond the reach of most parents' means. Of course we were always half promised one 'for Christmas' and failing that 'for your birthday' and then 'for Easter' and then 'for the Summer'. It never materialized, but we continued to hope and make believe with the following rhyme, which is still very popular although children today get 'two-wheelers' almost without asking.

I've a bike,
A fairy-bike,
I only got it
Last Saturday night.
I went up the hill,
Down the hill,
Under the arch,
And a rainbow.

For the first four lines the ball is just thrown against the wall and caught. But for the next lines:

I went up the hill: The ball is hopped from the ground to the wall then caught.
Down the hill: The ball is thrown against the wall and allowed to hop off the ground once before being caught.
Under the arch: The child stands with feet apart, then she hops the ball from behind, between her legs, and on to the wall.
And a rainbow: While the ball is in flight a rainbow is described in mid-air with the two hands.

63

The following verses can be played with one or two balls at a time. They can be accompanied by any or all of the various actions described, or indeed by any other action devised to make competition keener and call for greater skill. For example, having completed the usual run of actions like *Downy, Dashy, Right leg,* etc. it may be required to go through the whole thing again but using only one hand, first the right and then to make it more difficult still, the left.

Plainy marmalade,
Plainy marmalade.
One of the nurses
Lost her purses,
Plainy marmalade.

—◆—

Plainy packet of Rinso,
Over packet of Rinso,
Downy packet of Rinso,
Dashy packet of Rinso,
Right leg packet of Rinso,
Left leg packet of Rinso,
Archy packet of Rinso,
Backy packet of Rinso.

—◆—

Mrs. Dunne made her bun,
In the middle of a nun.
Saw a ghost eating toast,
Half-way up a lamp-post.

—◆—

Dolly, Dolly, had no sense,
She bought an egg for twenty cents.
The egg was bad,
Dolly went mad,
Dolly, Dolly, had no sense.

—◆—

Please get off the grass, Sir,
To let the ladies pass, Sir.
Ladies before gents, Sir,
So please get off the grass, Sir.

Yellow, yellow,[1]
What's for yellow.
Yellow is the colour
Of the fairy's umbrella.

—◆—

Ten and ten are twenty
Give the fox plenty

—◆—

Minnie the witch
She thought she was rich,
Because she found a ha'penny
In a bundle of sticks.

—◆—

Johnny had a gun,
And the gun was loaded.
Johnny pulled the trigger
And the gun exploded.

—◆—

Tiger Tim
He swallowed a pin,
And that's the end
Of Tiger Tim.

—◆—

My sister Eileen and I fell out,
I'll tell you what it was all about:
She liked coffee,
And I liked tea,
And that's the reason
We couldn't agree.

—◆—

Mrs. Brown,
Went to town,
With one leg up,
And the other leg down.

[1] *Yellow* pronounced *yella* to rhyme with *umbrella*.

The following two verses are of recent origin.

> Mary Mac, Mac, Mac,
> She dressed in black, black, black.
> Silver buttons, buttons, buttons,
> On her back, back, back.
> She asked her mother, mother, mother,
> Could she have sixty cents, cents, cents,
> To see the elephant, elephant, elephant,
> Jump the high, high, fence.
> He jumped so high, high, high,
> He reached the sky, sky, sky,
> And he came back, back, back,
> To Mary Mac, Mac, Mac.

—◇—

> Are you the lad,
> That hit the lad,
> The lad around the corner?
> Come back my lad,
> And tell the lad,
> That you're the lad,
> That hit the lad,
> The lad around the corner.

BILLY BOLAND

This is another *ball against the wall* game but instead of playing with just one ball, two or three balls are kept in play like a juggler while you say:

> Billy Boland
> Biscuit Baker
> Ballybough[1] bridge.

You then proceed to *steadies, right foot, left foot,* as in the previous game.

The other major city bakeries have also been honoured by rhymes used for hopping a ball.

---

[1] Pronounced *Ballybock.*

Johnston Mooney and O'Brien,
Bought a horse for one and nine.
When the horse began to kick,
Johnston Mooney bought a stick.
When the stick began to wear,
Johnston Mooney began to swear.
When the swear began to stop,
Johnston Mooney bought a shop.
When the shop began to sell,
Johnston Mooney went to Hell.

———◇———

Don't eat Kennedy's bread,
It'll fill your belly full of lead.
You'll fart like thunder,
Your mother wouldn't wonder,
Don't eat Kennedy's bread.

Children also have a habit of calling out these verses when they see the delivery-van of one of these bakeries passing.

QUEENIE

Any number over three can play, the more the better. The child who is 'Queenie' stands with her back to all the other children. She throws the ball over her head to them. If one of them catches the ball before it touches the ground she becomes 'Queenie', but not without a little extra measure of fun. As soon as she catches the ball, she sneaks up quietly behind 'Queenie' and proceeds to throw the ball over her head to the others, much to their delight and to 'Queenie's' disgust when she discovers it. If she doesn't add this extra bit she simply calls out *Caught ball eye o*. If the ball is not caught this way, there's usually a scramble for it and the child who gets it hides it behind her back. Then they all call out *Queenie eye o* or they chant the following verse:

Queenie eye o,
Who has the ball?
Is she small or is she tall?

'Queenie' turns around and if she guesses correctly who has the ball, she's still 'Queenie'. If she doesn't, it's the turn of the child who has the ball.

DONKEY

Three or more can play. They stand in a triangle or square according to the number taking part and the ball is thrown from one to the other in order. Sometimes to make it more exciting it's thrown to anyone at random. If one fails to catch the ball she merits a D, the next time O and so on until one of the players is DONKEY. Having become 'Donkey' the child is eliminated.
The last one wins the game.

Skipping

A child may have a rope all to herself, but she seldom if ever skips for very long on her own. As soon as another child appears she will turn her solo skipping into a game by inviting the other child into the rope with her, chanting:

> I call in my sister – (*Name*)

She mentions the name only of the child, e.g. Mary, and Mary runs into the rope to join her. Then skipping together she continues (to the same air as the last four lines of tune on p. 82)

> Oh! Mary,
> My bonny, bonny, Mary,
> All the boys and all the girls,
> They love Mary.

There may be a third child present who will run into the back of the rope and make skipping together more difficult, but more fun.
So as soon as there are three to play skipping you'll find the number increases every minute so that a large rope with two children turning it is needed.
When the skipping season comes around in the spring, the distinctive sounds associated with it dominate the air: the slap-slap of the

skipping-rope on the ground and the rhythmic clamping of feet mingling with the young voices chanting out the various rhymes. It is mostly the girls who play skipping. Ocasionally the boys may be persuaded to join in or to turn the rope.

Nobody ever volunteers to turn the rope, so in order to give everybody a fair chance, the following method of deciding who will turn is used:

> One of the girls takes the rope and bending her left arm she coils the rope round her elbow and the palm of her hand, concealing the two ends well. Each child takes a loop and whoever gets the loops nearest the ends are 'on it'.

The older children *run into* the rope and *run out* of it while it's turning. The younger ones are allowed to *stand to it*. For this the rope is kept still, a few inches from the ground. After counting *one, two, three* or *ready, steady, go,* it is turned.

The child who causes the rope to stop either by missing a step or maybe running in on the wrong step or just catching the hem of her skirt on the rope as she runs out, must take her chance at turning the rope. If the two turning the rope decide they've been left turning it a little too long they may decide to *chuck* the rope; that is, they give it a short sharp pull so that someone is bound to get caught. They do this when there's a crowd in together so that it may not be noticed, but it often is, and the result can be a terrible row.

It will be noted that in the various skipping rhymes use is made of counting in fives (5, 10, 15, 20, etc.) and of the alphabet. Also games like *Flowers, Trees, Colours, Fruit,* provide an easy way of learning the names of a very wide variety of these. But, more important to the children perhaps is the way they can freely mention such delectable items as 'sugary candy', 'apple jelly', 'ice cream', 'bluebells and cockle shells' and 'pancakes'.

Many of the verses have been brought up to date with the mention of the more recent housing estate at Finglas, and Television Commercials:

> Ask your mother to buy Lyons Tea
> *or*
> Ask Annie Oakley to buy Lyons Tea
> *or*
> We will take her off T.V.

Another feature which recurs in many of the verses is the use of the same kind of ending:

O-U-T spells Out *or* I must not miss a loop-ee-o.

Another such ending is:

Echo, echo, G-O Go!

CHASE, CHASE

Having decided who is to turn the rope, the next step is to see that everyone gets warmed up by getting a quick and frequent chance in the rope. And the best game for this is *Chase, Chase*. For this the rope is turned at a smart pace and the children run in one after the other. Each one skips once and runs out and then the next child comes in never 'missing a loop'. Anyone who misses is out and must take her turn at turning the rope. While they are running into, and out of, the rope, the following verse is chanted repeatedly:

Chase, chase, chase the baldy elephant,
That never told a lie on (*Name*)[1]
That was (*Name*).

Sometimes the following line only may be chanted repeatedly with no names mentioned:

Chase, chase, chase, the fox.

---

[1] The name and surname of the child who is in the rope at this point is called out.

DRIP, DROP

The following is done in much the same way as *Chase, Chase,* except
that each child skips twice in the rope then runs out:

> Drip, drop, dropping in the sea,
> (*or* The sailors on the sea)
> Please take the rope from me.
> Are you coming to the fair?
> No, no, the fair's not there.
> (With your) I must not miss a loop-ee-o.

Swinging on a lamp-post is a very dangerous 'sport' and a policeman
is sure to demand the removal of the rope or indeed he may remove
it himself, if he catches you out. This lends an element of excitement
and may be part of its fascination, for no law or awareness of
danger has so far succeeded in eliminating the practice. So we have
the following skipping rhyme:

> Drip, drop, the sailors on the sea,
> They are looking for a girl like me.
> Because I was swinging on the lamp,
> They took my address and sent it to my aunt,
> With your I must not miss a loop-ee-o.

FLOWERS

The two who are to turn the rope each choose the name of a flower,
each telling the other in a whisper what her choice is. The other
players form a line and the rope is turned. As each one runs into the

20. In fact a swing can be erected anywhere

21. Jumps (p. 99)

22. Standing hopefully by helping to swing the rope (p. 10)

23. Once there is chalk to be had no surface escapes (p. 44)

rope she names a flower and goes out again. The one who names the flower chosen by one of those turning the rope must now take her place at turning the rope and decide with her partner on another flower. This game can also be played with the names of Fruit, Colours, Countries, or Trees.

—◇—

With the following rhymes each child gets a long skip. She skips on her own for the length of the rhyme then runs out and the next child gets her chance.

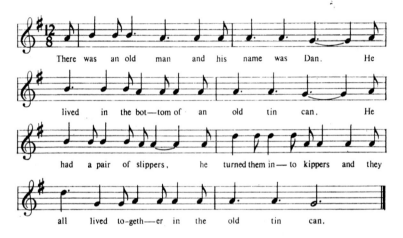

There was an old man, and his name was Dan. He lived in the bot—tom of an old tin can. He had a pair of slippers, he turned them in—to kippers and they all lived to-geth—er in the old tin can.

There was an old man,
And his name was Dan.
He lived in the bottom
Of an old tin can.
He had a pair of slippers,
(And) he turned them into kippers,
And they all lived together
In the old tin can.

—◇—

There was a little man
And he had a little gun,
And up the chimney he did run;
With his belly full of fat,
And an old tall hat,
And a pancake tied
To his bum, bum, bum.

—◇—

Willie Willie Wagtail
Born in an egg-shell
Christened in a teacup
Died in a dung-cart
That was the end of poor Willie Wagtail.

—◇—

Ash Wednes-day, Shrove Tues —day, when Jack went to school, his mo-ther made pan—cakes and she left them to cool. She roast them, she toast them, she made them so hot, she put too much pepper on them, and she pois—oned poor Jack.

Ash Wednesday, Shrove Tuesday,
When Jack went to school,
His mother made pancakes,
And she left them to cool.
She roast them, she toast them,
She made them so hot,
She put too much pepper on them,
And she poisoned poor Jack.

The following verse has the same air:

Shrove Tuesday, Shrove Tuesday,
When Jack went to school,
His mother made pancakes,
Without any gruel.
She tossed them, she turned them,
She made them so black,
And she put so much pepper on
That she poisoned poor Jack.

—◆—

Two little fleas[1]
Got fourteen days
For hopping on a Jewman's back.
The Jewman swore,
If he got them any more,
That he'd break every bone
In their back.

—◆—

I had a box of chocolates,
I left them on the shelf.
Would you believe?
Would you believe?
It walked away itself.
It might have been a fairy,
It might have been a queen,
It might have been a little girl
All dressed in green.

—◆—

A-B-C-D-E-F-G,
H-I-J-K-L-M-N,
O-P-Q-R-S-T-U,
V-W-X-Y-Z.
X-Y-Z,
Sugar on your bread,
Porridge in the morning,
Cocoa going to bed.

—◆—

[1] *Fleas* pronounced *flays* to rhyme with *days*.

75

ALL IN! ALL IN!

A-B-C-D-E-F-G,
H-I-J-K-L-M-N,
O-P-Q-R-S-T-U,
V-W-X-Y-Z.
X-Y-Z,
Sugar on your bread,
Go to the doctor
Before you're dead.

———◆———

I saw Esau
Sitting on a see-saw.
O-U-T spells Out.

———◆———

Keep it boiling,
On the glimmer
If you don't
You won't get your dinner.
Go home and tell your mother,
You lost your baby brother.
I lost him in the bed,
With a 'H' on his head.
North, South, East and West,
Cadbury's chocolates are the best.

———◆———

Keep it boiling,
On the glimmer,
If you don't
You won't get your dinner.
North, South, East and West
Cadbury's chocolates are the best.

Have a piece of barley-o,
Barley-o, barley-o.
Have a piece of barley-o,
Fresh sugary candy.

The following five verses have become very popular in recent years.

Jinny on the telephone,
Miss your loop you're out.
O-U-T spells Out.

Drip, drop, the sailors on the sea,
Ask Annie Oakley to buy Lyons tea.
If she doesn't buy Lyons tea,
We will take her off T.V.
With your I must not miss a loop-ee-o.

Drip, drop, the sailors on the sea,
Ask your mother to buy Lyons tea.
If she doesn't buy Lyons tea,
Please take the rope from me.
With your I must not miss a loop-ee-o.

Little black doctor
How is your wife?
Very well thank you
She's all right.
She won't eat lickerish (licorice)
Sticky old lickerish,
O-U-T spells Out.

77

ALL IN! ALL IN!

Mademoiselle,
Went to the well,
And didn't forget
Her soap and towel.
She washed her hands,
She wiped them dry,
She said her prayers,
And she went away.

—◆—

SALT, MUSTARD

The rope is first turned at a normal pace, then gets progressively faster until the skipper stops, then it is her turn to turn the rope.

Salt, mustard, ginger, cayenne,
Vinegar, salt, pepper.

I CALL IN

A variation of lone skipping is for the child to 'call in' the next in line before she actually finishes. They skip together for a while then the first one goes out. Variety is introduced with verses like *Bluebells, cockle shells*.

—◆—

Somebody under the bed
Whoever can it be,
I feel so very nervous
I call for (*Name*) in.
(*Name*) lights a candle,
Nobody there.
I die didily[1] i, and
Out goes she.

[1]*didily: id* as in *did*.

Somebody under the bed. Who---ev ---er can it be, I feel so ve---ry ner---vous, I call for Ma---ry in. Ma---ry lights a can--dle. no----body there. I die didily i. and out goes she.

Keep the kettle boiling
(Or) you won't get your tea.
When it's ready
Call for (*Name*).

Keep the ket–tle boil–ing, you won't get your tea. When it's ready call for Kathleen.

A boy stood on a burning deck,
A leg of mutton around his neck,
Who'll come in to save his life?
I will.

The boy stood on a burning deck,
His feet were full of blisters.
His father was in the public house,
And the beer ran down his whiskers.

———◇———

The boy stood on a burning deck,
His feet were full of blisters.
He burnt a hole in the seat of his pants,
And had to wear his sister's.

79

Vote, vote, vote for Mary Rei-lly. In comes Cora at the door eye O. Co-ra is the one that'll have a bit of fun and we don't want Mary a-ny more.

> Vote, vote, vote,
> For (*Name*)
> In comes (*Name*) at the door eye o.
> *(Name)* is the one
> That'll have a bit of fun,
> And we don't want *(Name)* any more.

That verse has never diminished in popularity, due perhaps to its distinctive tune. We used to chant:

> Vote, vote, vote for De Valera,

and I was surprised and delighted to hear the same words chanted on the third of February this year by five little girls aged between three and five years.

---◆---

The following verse is only known for the past six or seven years:

> Look who's coming down the street,
> *(Name)* on her feet.
> She was married twice before,
> Now she's knocking at *(Name)* door.
> *(Name, Name)* will you marry me?
> Yes love, yes love, at half past three.

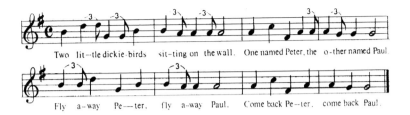

Two little dickie-birds (*or* blackbirds)
Sitting on the wall.
One named Peter,
The other named Paul.
Fly away Peter,
Fly away Paul.
Come back Peter,
Come back Paul.

The following verse has the same tune, but this time the actual names of the children are called out:

Two little sandy girls
On the sea-shore.
One named *(Name)*,
The other named *(Name)*.
Don't cry *(Name)*,
Don't cry *(Name)*,
Come in *(Name)*,
Good-bye *(Name)*.

———◆———

Two little sausages
Frying on the pan.
One got burned,
And the other said – scram!

81

Mother, Mother, I feel sick,
Send for the Doctor quick, quick, quick.
Doctor, Doctor, will I die,
Yes, my child and so will I.
How many carriages will I have,
5, 10, 15, 20, etc.

At the count of 5, 10, 15, etc., the rope is turned faster and faster until
the two who are skipping are forced to stop. Then they both must take
their chance to turn the rope.

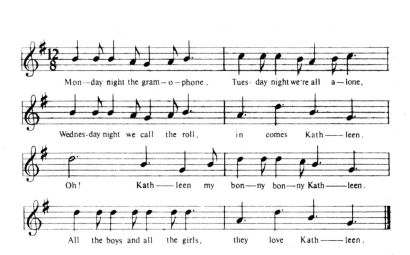

Monday night the gramophone,
Tuesday night we're all alone,
Wednesday night we call the roll,
In comes *(Name)*
Oh! *(Name)*
My bonny, bonny, *(Name)*
All the boys, and all the girls,
They love *(Name)*.

Positions are slightly reversed in this next verse:

Each child gets only a short skip in the rope at a time because at the word *push*, the next in line comes into the rope and pushes her out.

> Down in Nelson's Pillar
> Where the boat goes *push*.
> Everybody knows
> Where the boat goes *push*.

It will be interesting to see how long more the words Nelson's Pillar will survive in that skipping verse, since the once famous land-mark no longer exists, having been blown up in 1966.

BLUEBELLS

For the first two lines of the next verse the rope is rocked to and fro a short distance from the ground. The child whose turn it is jumps over it in time with the words. At the word *over* ordinary skipping is resumed.

> Bluebells, cockle-shells,
> Ee-ver, eye-ver, over,
> Mammy in the kitchen,
> Doing a bit of stitching
> In comes the beggar-man
> And out goes I.

ACTION RHYMES

The following *Action Rhymes* are performed by one child at a time. As in the previous section, variety is introduced with verses like *German Boys, Handy Andy* and *Ee-ver, eye-ver*.

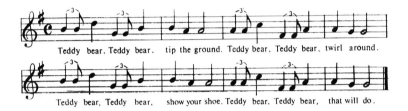

Teddy bear, Teddy bear. tip the ground. Teddy bear, Teddy bear, twirl around.

Teddy bear, Teddy bear, show your shoe. Teddy bear, Teddy bear, that will do.

> Teddy bear, teddy bear,
> Tip the ground.
> Teddy bear, teddy bear,
> Twirl around.
> Teddy bear, teddy bear,
> Show your shoe.
> Teddy bear, teddy bear,
> That will do.
> Teddy bear, teddy bear,
> Go up the stairs.
> Teddy bear, teddy bear,
> Say your prayers.
> Teddy bear, teddy bear,
> Put out the light.
> Teddy bear, teddy bear,
> Say good night.

Another version of this has 'Ladybird', instead of 'Teddy Bear' and finishes after eight lines of the above version with 'Please run through' instead of 'That will do'.

SKIPPING

Charlie Chaplin
Went to France,
To teach the ladies
How to dance.
And this is the way
He taught them:
First you do your cross-bars,
Then you do your kicks.
Then you do your twirl-around,
And then you do your splits.

At *cross-bars* she must cross her feet; at *kicks* she must kick out one leg; at *twirl-around* she must twirl right around skipping all the time; at *splits* she stops with the rope between her feet.

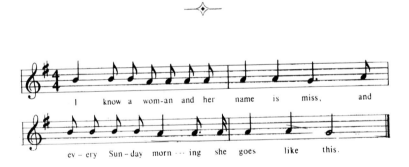

I know a woman
And her name is Miss,
And every Sunday morning
She goes like this.
(*or* She does the splits).

On the last word all come to a stand-still with the rope between their feet.

The following verses have become popular in the past eight or nine years.

> I'm a little girl guide
> All dressed in blue,
> These are the actions I can do:
> Salute to your officer,
> Bow to your queen,
> And run around the corner
> Before you're seen.
> (*or* To buy an ice cream).

—◆—

> Jelly on a plate,
> Jelly on a plate,
> Wibbly wobbly, wibbly wobbly,[1]
> Jelly on a plate.

> Sausage on the pan,
> Sausage on the pan,
> Turn it over, turn it over[2]
> Sausage on the pan.

> Money on the floor,
> Money on the floor,
> Pick it up, pick it up,[3]
> Money on the floor.

> Robbers in the house,
> Robbers in the house,
> Will you kick them out,[4]
> Kick them out,
> Robbers in the house.

[1] At this the child wriggles her body while still skipping.
[2] At this the child keeps turning around while still skipping.
[3] At this the child bends down to tip the ground.
[4] At this the child kicks one foot out in front of her.

GERMAN BOYS

One child at a time goes into the rope. She skips in the centre for the first two lines:

> German boys are not so funny
> This is the way they count their money.

Then from a penny to a shilling is counted out with the following actions:

One penny: She skips into the rope then runs quickly around one of the girls turning the rope and is ready to skip into the rope again for:

Two pennies: Having skipped once, she runs around again and back for:

Three pennies: For this she runs *under* the rope and around again.

Four pennies and *five pennies:* The same as for *one* and *two*.

Six pennies: The same as for *three*.

Seven pennies and *eight pennies:* The same as for *one* and *two*.

Nine Pennies: The same as for *three*.

Ten pennies and *eleven pennies:* The same as for *one* and *two*.

A shilling: The same as for *three*.

That game became popular about eight years ago.

HANDY ANDY

One child at a time stands into the rope which is raised above her head. She crouches down to avoid being struck. The rope is turned above her head while the first two lines are recited, then normal skipping is resumed.

> Handy Andy sugary candy,
> Fresh enarmel (carmel) rock.
> I spy a lark,
> Shining in the dark,
> Echo, echo, G-O. Go!

UP THE LADDER

The skipper must go from one end of the rope to the other to illustrate going up the ladder and down the spout. For the last lines 'John came out', etc. she stays in the centre of the rope.

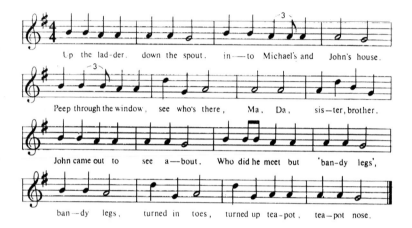

Up the ladder, down the spout,
Into Michael's and John's house.
Peep through the window,
See who's there,
Ma, Da, sister, brother.
John came out to see about,
Who did he meet but 'bandy-legs',
Bandy legs, turned in toes,
Turned up teapot, teapot, nose.

EE-VER, EYE-VER

This is performed in the same way as *Bluebells*, but at the words 'My little rope', etc. the rope is not only turned over but the two who are turning the rope move around in a clockwise direction while they

24. Mowl (p. 38)

25. Lifting open the small cover of the water hydrant and aiming coins into it (p. 38)

26. The amount
of concentration
spent on each
throw is amazing
(p. 33)

27. A player may land his coin directly into the mowl (p. 38)

turn, so that it is more difficult for the skipper to stay in the centre of the rope.

Ee-ver, eye-ver, chimney sweeper,
Had a wife and could not keep her.
Had another, did not love her,
Up the chimney he did put her.
Mammy in the butchers buying a pound of beef,
Baby in the cradle fast asleep.
My little rope must turn over.
With a rick-a-rock, a rick-a-rock,
A rick-a-rock-a-rover,
Rick-a-rock, a rick-a-rock
A rick-a-rock-a-rover.

A CHANGE OF TUNE

In the following group the rhymes are much longer, and being for
older girls there is a complete change of sentiment. One girl at a time
goes into the rope, while the others line up at the side chanting the
verse until their own turn comes round.

APPLE JELLY

One child at a time skips while all the others call out the questions
and answers. It begins with the sing-song lines of *Apple Jelly:*

App – le   jel --ly   my jam tart,   tell me the name of   your sweetheart.

> Apple jelly my jam-tart,
> Tell me the name of your sweetheart.
> A-B-C-D-E, etc.

The alphabet is then called out, and repeated if necessary, the pace
getting progressively faster until the skipper stops. Whichever letter
is reached when she stops, this is the initial of her sweetheart. Then
follow the various other questions and possible answers.

> What will your sweetheart be?
> > A tinker, a tailor,
> > A soldier, a sailor,
> > A rich man, a poor man,
> > A beggar-man, a thief.

These names are repeated, the pace getting progressively faster as
before, until the skipper stops. The name she stops at, this is what
her sweetheart will be. She will, however, always take care that she
doesn't stop at either *a poor man, a beggar-man* or *a thief!* All the
other questions are decided in the same way.

Will you marry him?

    Yes, no, certainly so.

When will you marry him?

    January, February, etc.

The months of the year are called out until the skipper stops.

What dress will you wear?

    Silk, satin, muslin, rags.

What will you wear on your feet?

    Boots, shoes, slippers or clogs.

What will you go to church in?

    A coach, a carriage or an ass and cart.

How many children will you have?

    Five, ten, fifteen, twenty, etc.

You will notice that even for a question such as this last one, the common practice of counting in fives is continued.

DOWN BY THE RIVER

Down by the river where the green grass grows. Where Mary Kel—ly washes all her clothes, she sang and she sang and she sang so sweet, she called for her sweetheart down the street. Sweetheart, sweetheart, will you marry me? Yes love, yes love, at half past three. Ice cake, jam cake, all for tea and we'll all be together at half past three.

ALL IN! ALL IN!

Down by the river
Where the green grass grows.
Where *(Name)*
Washes all her clothes,
She sang, and she sang,
And she sang so sweet,
She called for her sweetheart
Down the street.
Sweetheart, sweetheart,
Will you marry me,
Yes love, yes love,
At half past three.
Ice cake, jam cake,
All for tea,
And we'll all be together
At half past three.

Other versions of the last four lines are:

Jam pies, apple pies,
All for tea,
And we're going to have a great time
At half past three.

Half past three is
Much too late,
So we'll be married
At half past eight.

—◇—

The rain, the rain,
The rain blew high,
The rain came tumbling
From the sky.
(Name) said she'd die
If she didn't get the fellow
With the marble eye.
She is handsome, she is pretty,

She is a girl from Dublin City.
All the boys say they love her,
All the boys are fighting for her,
Let them say what e'er they like,
(Name) is my wife.

The rain. the rain. the rain blew high. the rain came tumbling from the sky.

No-ra Whe-lan said she'd die if she didn't get the fellow with the marble eye

She is handsome she is pret-ty she is the girl from Dub-lin Ci-ty

All the boys say they love her, all the boys are fighting for her.

Let them say what-e'er they like. for No-ra Whe-lan is my wife.

When the houses of a new Corporation scheme are ready for occupation, some families in older schemes like to transfer to one of these new houses. This is particularly so when the new scheme is on the same side of the river Liffey. Therefore in any new Corporation housing estate you find people from many areas of the city. Those I have just mentioned who choose to transfer from an older scheme, those who come from condemned tenements in the city centre and are living in the suburbs for the first time, and young couples who had been living with parents until they had the necessary three children in order to qualify for one of these houses. So, children from all parts of the city find themselves playing together in new and strange surroundings. But they bring with them to these new surroundings their street-games and rhymes which act as a unifying element among them. When the scheme at Finglas in North East Dublin was completed, some families from our area transferred to it. The older children of these families continued for some time to come back to The Park to visit their friends and join in the street-games. It was these children who brought to The Park the last four lines of the following rhyme. These were added it seems by common consent, as it were, to bring Finglas into the rhyme as much as the rhyme had been brought to Finglas.

> Monday is my washing day,
> Tuesday I'm alone.
> Wednesday is my ironing day,
> And I hope my fellow comes.
> He didn't come last Wednesday,
> Nor the Wednesday before,
> If he doesn't come this Wednesday,
> He needn't come any more.
> Johnny gives me apples,
> Johnny gives me pears,
> Johnny gives me sixpence
> To kiss him on the stairs.
> The stairs went crack,
> Johnny broke his back,
> And all the ducks in Finglas
> Went quack! quack! quack!

This following rhyme became known in The Park for the first time about ten years ago.

> Once I had the measles
> I had them very long,
> My mother wrapped me in a blanket
> And threw me in the pram.
> The pram was very shaky,
> I nearly tumbled out,
> My mother brought me to hospital,
> And hear the baby shout:
> Mammy! Daddy!
> Take me home,

From this convalescent home.
I am here a week or two,
And now I want to stay with you.
Good-bye all the nurses,
Good-bye all the doctors,
And Sister Eithne too.

ALL IN TOGETHER

For the following verses all run into the rope together and skip in
unison while the verse is chanted. All must leave the rope together.

All in to—geth—er girls, this fine weather girls.

Get your hat and get your coat and get your um—ber—el——la girls.

I spy a lark. shin—ing in the dark.

Ech——o, ech——o, G. O., GO!

All in together girls,
This fine weather girls,
Get your hat, and get your coat,
And get your umbrella girls.
I spy a lark, shining in the dark,
Echo, echo, G-O, GO!

—◇—

All in together girls,
This fine weather girls,
I spy a lark, shining in the dark,
Out goes one,
Out goes two,
Out goes the little girl
All dressed in blue.

—◇—

Ice-cream a penny a lump,
The more you eat
The more you jump.

—◇—

I scream, you scream,
We all scream
For ice-cream

—◇—

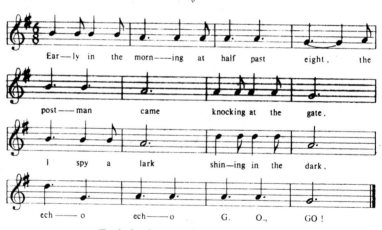

Ear—ly in the morn——ing at half past eight, the post——man came knocking at the gate. I spy a lark shin—ing in the dark, ech——o ech——o G. O., GO !

Early in the morning
At half past eight,
The postman came
Knocking at the gate.
I spy a lark,
Shining in the dark,
Echo, echo, G-O, GO!

—◇—

96

Hot cross buns,
Hot cross buns,
One a penny,
Two a penny,
Hot cross buns.

———◆———

Goosey goosey gander,
Where do you wander.
Upstairs, downstairs,
In my lady's chamber.
There I met an old man
Who wouldn't say his prayers,
I caught him by the left leg,
And threw him down the stairs.

———◆———

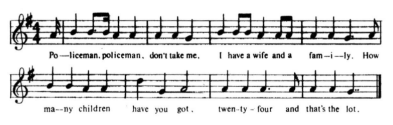

Po—liceman, policeman, don't take me.   I have a wife and a   fam—i—ly. How

ma—ny children   have you got,   twen-ty - four   and that's the lot.

Policeman, policeman, don't take me,
I have a wife and a family.
How many children have you got,
Twenty-four and that's the lot.

And a very recent version of this is:

Inspector, inspector, don't take me
And I'll pay my fare to the C.I.E.[1]

This was probably composed on the spot one day by a child who was
caught trying to dodge paying his bus fare.

[1]   Córas Iompair Éireann (The Irish Transport System).

ALL IN! ALL IN!

Cobbler, cobbler, mend my shoe,
Have it done by half past two.
Tick-tack, tick-tack, tick-tack-too.

No more Irish,
No more French,
No more sitting on the hard school bench.
Bang on the tables,
Break up the chairs,
And throw old (*Name*)[1]
Down the stairs.

(*Name*) is a very good man,
He tries to teach us all he can.
Reading, writing, arithmetic,
He never forgets to use the stick.

(*Name*) is a very good man,
He goes to Mass on Sunday,
And prays to God to give him strength
To bash the kids on Monday.

(*Name*)[2] is no good,
Chop him up for fire-wood.
If he doesn't do for that,
Give him to the pussy-cat.

Our school is a very good school,
It's made of sticks and plaster.
The only thing that's wrong with it,
Is the baldy-headed master.

[1] The surname or nickname of the school-teacher.
[2] The name of a school-teacher or a child.

FRENCH SKIPPING

In *French Skipping* two matching ropes are used, or a very long rope is doubled in two. Each child turns clockwise with the left hand rope, and anti-clockwise with the right hand rope, alternately. This requires very fast skipping and no rhyme is sung during it, for it takes all one's concentration to avoid tripping up.

JUMPS

Apart from skipping, a rope is also used for playing *Jumps*. The preliminaries are the same as for skipping, two are picked to hold the rope while the others line up. The rope is first raised an inch or two above the ground and each child jumps over it. Anyone failing to jump clear of the rope is out. Gradually it is raised higher and higher and of course each time the number of children going on to the next round gets smaller, the last one in, wins the game. This year for the first time I noticed boys playing this game on their own. Usually *Jumps* are played by both boys and girls together. Another jump game played with a rope needs only one child to hold the rope aloft with one hand. Usually the tallest child offers to hold the rope. She then turns the rope around maypole-fashion, keeping the end a certain distance from the ground. Each child jumps over it as it comes her way, anyone failing to jump clear is out.

Another game played with a rope goes like this: Two children hold the rope as for *Jumps*. But this time they can decide to hold it so high the children run under the rope saying *Under the moon*, or they may lower it so that they jump over it saying *Over the stars*.

Portraits of Life

The sing-song verses of the following games or *Portraits of Life* are as much a harbinger of summer to Dubliners as the cuckoo is to the countryman. These little portraits are usually played with the boys and girls standing in a circle holding hands while they move around singing the verse. The central figure stands in the middle of the ring. The story to be enacted is always such that most of the children in the ring get a chance to play some part in the game without too much delay—or, as in the case of *Stands a Lady* where there are two 'central' figures involved, who have such spectacular parts to play, it is worth waiting for your chance. As the days get longer and warmer, circles of various sizes are seen and the never-changing verses are heard echoing the same sentiments that our mothers and grandmothers sang. Children who last year could hardly talk, are this year included in a circle for the first time and initiated into the strange world of the mysterious lady who stands on the mountain still seeking *gold and silver and a nice young man,* and the farmer who is still looking for a wife.

Other games are played with the children divided into two parts and lined up facing each other. Compared to the ring games these have a more direct approach. When *The Old Woman from Sandy Land* wants to get her daughters settled, she just lines them up and without any preamble states her case and describes their various accomplishments. And she has no trouble disposing of them. Likewise when *The King of Rifles* arrives looking for a wife he straightforwardly picks the fairest one and goes off with her. Oddly enough the gipsy is much more choosey. He finds fault with the maidens and they of course answer back and the gipsy ends up with no wife at all. The soldier just back from the war being out of touch with the ladies may have got off to a bad start by singing his own praises first. Anyhow when he discovers that his wealth is his only attraction, he rejects all the maidens offered to him. I have always felt very sorry for the soldier. But there always seems a greater element of magic and excitement about the ring games. They offer a wider variety of entertainment, singing and miming and chasing and guessing.

One such game is *I sent a letter* . . . The chase at the end is like *The Cat and the Mouse*[1] and causes great excitement for all. In *Wallflowers* your name is called according to your age but in *The Darkie Bluebells* you could be picked to join the chain at any moment depending on the size of the circle, and where you are standing, at the end of the verse. So there is more excitement, and this is maintained right up to the end when the whole chain breaks up in laughter and confusion.

Then there is the age-old problem of getting *Lazy Mary* out of bed. First she is coaxed with all the things likely to entice her. Here again scope is allowed for indulging any particular longing one may have. Eventually when the coaxing fails 'Mary' is threatened with the cane and gets up.

THE FARMER WANTS A WIFE

The boys and girls holding hands, move around clock-wise singing the verse, while one child, the 'Farmer', goes around anti-clock-wise inside the circle with his eyes closed. He picks out a 'Wife', then the wife picks a 'Child' and so on. In the end all gather around the 'Bone' beating him on the back and chanting *The bone won't crack*. The verses commencing *Pick a nice* . . . are not always included.

The farm-er wants a wife. the farm-er wants a wife.

Ee eye, ee eye, the farm-er wants a wife.

[1] See p. 161.

ALL IN! ALL IN!

The farmer wants a wife,
The farmer wants a wife,
Ee eye, ee eye, the farmer wants a wife.

Pick a nice wife,
Pick a nice wife,
Eee eye, ee eye, pick a nice wife.

The wife wants a child,
The wife wants a child,
Ee eye, ee eye, the wife wants a child.

Pick a nice child,
Pick a nice child,
Ee eye, ee eye, pick a nice child.

The child wants a dog,
The child wants a dog,
Ee eye, ee eye, the child wants a dog.

Pick a nice dog,
Pick a nice dog,
Ee eye, ee eye, pick a nice dog.

The dog wants a bone,
The dog wants a bone,
Ee eye, ee eye, the dog wants a bone.

Pick a nice bone,
Pick a nice bone,
Ee eye, ee eye, pick a nice bone.

The bone won't crack,
The bone won't crack,
Ee eye, ee eye, the bone won't crack.

STANDS A LADY

A girl stands in the centre of the ring and the other girls and boys
hold hands and move around singing:

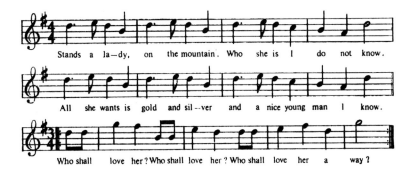

Stands a lady, on the mountain,
Who she is I do not know.
All she wants is gold and silver,
And a nice young man I know.
Who shall love her?
Who shall love her?
Who shall love her away?
Who shall love her?
Who shall love her?
Who shall love her away?

She picks one of the children from the ring for her 'Young Man' and holding hands they ask to get out of the ring saying:

Open the gates and let me through!

The others reply:

Not till you show your black and blue!

The couple then put forward their right foot then their left foot saying:

There's my black,
And there's my blue,
So open the gates and let me through!

The gates are opened and they go out of the ring and perform the various acts, as sung by those in the ring (to the air of the last five bars).

103

Go to church, love, go to church, love,
Go to church, love, away.

Kneel down, love, kneel down, love,
Kneel down, love, away.

Say your prayers, love, say your prayers, love,
Say your prayers, love, away.

Put on your ring, love, put on your ring, love.
Put on your ring, love, away.

Stand up, love, stand up, love,
Stand up, love, away.

Go for a long walk, go for a long walk,
Go for a long walk, away.

Come home, love, come home, love,
Come home, love, away.

The two come 'home', but to get back into the ring they must go through the same routine as they did to get out.

The following version was given to me by a woman who heard it and saw it played in Liffey Street over fifty years ago and wrote it down at the time. The ritual is the same but the first verse differs from the one above:

Stands a lady, on the mountain,
Who she is I do not know.
All she wants is gold and silver,
All she wants is a nice young man.
Take her by the lily-white hand,
Take her across the water,
Give her a kiss and a one, two, three,
And then she's a lady's daughter.

Then they leave the ring and perform the various acts as before, but instead of *away* at the end of each act, in this version it's *farewell*. When the couple come back into the ring there is this extra verse to finish off the performance:

28. Scut the whip! (p. 25)

29. Then they may run off to the newsagents and knock down the placards outside (p. 24)

30. If she can get old high-heeled shoes so much the better (p. 28)

31. I call in (p. 78)

Now they're married and they're going to die.
First to a boy and second to a girl.
Seven years young and seven years old.
Now they're married, give a kiss and be done.

THE OLD WOMAN FROM SANDY LAND

The 'Old Woman' and her 'Children' pace back and forth in front
of the 'Man' singing the verse:

Here's the old woman from San—dy Land, with all her children by the hand.

One can knit, the other can sew, the other can make a li—ly-white bow. An-

other can make a dress for a queen, so please take one of my off——spring.

The fairest one that I can see is Mona Casey, come along with me.

There's poor Mo—na, she is gone, with out a far—thing in her hand.

All she has is a little gold band. Good-bye. Mona! Good—bye!

105

ALL IN! ALL IN!

> Here's the old woman from Sandy Land,
> With all her children by the hand.
> One can knit, the other can sew,
> The other can make a lily-white bow.
> Another can make a dress for a queen,
> So please take one of my offspring.
> (*or* one of my daughters)
> (*or* one of them off me)

The 'Man' replies with a different tune:

> The fairest one that I can see,
> Is (*Name*) come along with me.

The 'Old Woman' and her 'Children' continue:

> There's poor *(Name)* she is gone,
> Without a farthing in her hand.
> All she has is a little gold band,
> Good-bye *(Name)*! Good-bye!

The whole thing is repeated until all the daughters are gone.

HERE'S THE GIPSY RIDING

Any number can play. One is chosen as the 'Gipsy' and two others for his friends. These three stand on one side and all the others (the 'Ladies') stand facing them. To start off all move back and forth singing:

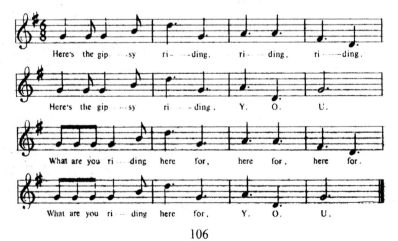

Here's the gip--sy ri--ding, ri--ding, ri--ding.
Here's the gip--sy ri--ding. Y. O. U.
What are you ri--ding here for, here for, here for.
What are you ri--ding here for. Y. O. U.

> Here's the gipsy riding, riding, riding,
> Here's the gipsy riding, Y-O-U.

Then the 'Ladies' approach the 'Gipsies' singing:

> What are you riding here for, here for, here for,
> What are you riding here for, Y-O-U.

The Gipsies reply:

> We're riding here to marry, marry, marry,
> We're riding here to marry, Y-O-U.

The Ladies:

> Marry one of us Sir, us Sir, us Sir,
> Marry one of us Sir, Y-O-U.

The Gipsies:

> You're all as stiff as pokers, pokers, pokers,
> You're all as stiff as pokers, Y-O-U.

They portray what they mean by appropriate actions.

The Ladies:

> We're not as stiff as you Sir, you Sir, you Sir,
> We're not as stiff as you Sir, Y-O-U.

They perform all sorts of actions like tipping their toes etc. to prove their point.

The Gipsies:

> You're all too dirty, dirty, dirty,
> You're all too dirty, Y-O-U.

They each stamp a foot at the word *dirty* for emphasis.

The Ladies:

> We're not as black as you Sir, you Sir, you Sir.
> We're not as black as you Sir, Y-O-U.

or

We're just as clean as you Sir, you Sir, you Sir,
We're just as clean as you Sir, Y-O-U.

For this they turn their backs on the 'Gipsies' and flick out the hems of their dresses in disdain. Then turning around to face them again they sing:

We wouldn't marry you Sir, you Sir, you Sir,
We wouldn't marry you Sir, Y-O-U.

As a variation the following verses may be substituted after the 'Gipsies' say: *We're riding here to marry . . .*

The Ladies:

Who're you going to marry, marry, marry,
Who're you going to marry, Y-O-U.

The 'Gipsies' decide on one of the girls, say, Carmel:

I'm going to marry Carmel, Carmel, Carmel,
I'm going to marry Carmel, Y-O-U.

The Ladies:

You can't have your Carmel, Carmel, Carmel,
You can't have your Carmel, Y-O-U.

The Gipsies:

I must have my Carmel, Carmel, Carmel,
I must have my Carmel, Y-O-U.

The Ladies:

There's your dirty Carmel, Carmel, Carmel,
There's your dirty Carmel, Y-O-U.

Carmel is given over to the 'Gipsies' and the game is repeated until all have been taken over by the 'Gipsies'.

THE KING OF RIFLES

This is another version of *Here's the Gipsy Riding*. It has the same air also for the first four verses, then the air changes, and at 'The fairest one . . .' it repeats the last part of *The Old Woman from Sandy Land* except that one line is omitted. The 'Ladies' form a straight line and the 'King of Rifles' stands in front of them while he sings:

King:

> I'm the King of Rifles, Rifles, Rifles,
> I'm the King of Rifles,
> Ee eye o.

Ladies:

> What do you want here Sir, here Sir, here Sir,
> What do you want here Sir,
> Ee eye o.

King:

> I want to marry, marry, marry,
> I want to marry,
> Ee eye o.

Ladies:

> Marry one of us Sir, us Sir, us Sir,
> Marry one of us Sir,
> Ee eye o.

King:

> The fairest one that I can see,
> Is *(Name)* come along with me.

Ladies:

> Now poor *(Name)* she is gone,
> Without a farthing in her hand,
> Good-bye *(Name)*! Good-bye!

And still another version goes:

> Here's the King arriving, arriving, arriving,
> Here's the King arriving, Y-O-U.

What are you arriving here for, here for, here for,
What are you arriving here for, Y-O-U.

I'm arriving here to marry, marry, marry,
I'm arriving here to marry, Y-O-U.

Then marry one of us Sir, us Sir, us Sir,
Then marry one of us Sir, Y-O-U.

CHINESE GOVERNOR

One child is chosen to be the 'Chinese Governor'. All the others
form a line and walk backwards and forwards in front of him saying:

Chinese Governor,
Blackman's daughter.
Tra la la la la,
It's a very fine day.
The wind blew high,
Over the sky,
And out walks *(Name)*.

Whichever child steps forward (because she is the youngest or the
oldest or just the first in the row) takes the hand of the 'Chinese
Governor' and they hop around saying the verse again. Then the
'Chinese Governor' goes back to the line and the other child becomes
'Governor' for the next game.

This game is only being played for the past five or six years.

WILL YOU MARRY

The children are divided into two rows. They face each other,
walking back and forth as they sing the alternate verses:

I'm a soldier brave and strong,
After coming from the war.
Will you marry, marry, marry, marry,
Will you marry me?

110

If you're a soldier brave and strong,
After coming from the war,
I won't marry, marry, marry, marry,
I won't marry you.

If I give you a golden ball,
To play with the gipsies in the hall,
Will you marry, marry, marry, marry,
Will you marry me?

If you give me a golden ball,
To play with the gipsies in the hall,
I won't marry, marry, marry, marry,
I won't marry you.

If I give you a golden spoon,
To feed the baby in the afternoon,
Will you marry, marry, marry, marry,
Will you marry me?

If you give me a golden spoon,
To feed the baby in the afternoon,
I won't marry, marry, marry, marry,
I won't marry you.

If I give you a piece of cake,
To throw to the swans in the lake,
Will you marry, marry, marry, marry,
Will you marry me?

If you give me a piece of cake,
To throw to the swans in the lake,
I won't marry, marry, marry, marry,
I won't marry you.

If I give you the keys of the press,
And all the money I possess,
Will you marry, marry, marry, marry,
Will you marry me?

If you give me the keys of the press,
And all the money you possess,
I *will* marry, marry, marry, marry,
I *will* marry you.

Well I *won't* give you the keys of the press,
And all the money I possess,
And I *won't* marry, marry, marry, marry,
I *won't* marry you.

THE ROMAN SOLDIERS

The more children for this the better, they are divided into two sides,
one the 'Irish Soldiers', the other the 'Roman (*or* the 'English')
Soldiers'.

Irish Soldiers:

> Will you have a glass of wine?
> Will you have a glass of wine?
> Will you have a glass of wine?
> We're the Irish Soldiers.

Roman Soldiers:

No, we won't have a glass of wine,
No, we won't have a glass of wine,
No, we won't have a glass of wine,
We're the Roman Soldiers.

Irish Soldiers:

Will you have a slice of cake?
Will you have a slice of cake?
Will you have a slice of cake?
We're the Irish Soldiers.

Roman Soldiers:

No, we won't have a slice of cake,
No, we won't have a slice of cake,
No, we won't have a slice of cake,
We're the Roman Soldiers.

Irish Soldiers:

Are you ready for a fight?
Are you ready for a fight?
Are you ready for a fight?
We're the Irish Soldiers.
or
Will you have a war with us?
Will you have a war with us?
Will you have a war with us?
We're the Irish Soldiers.

Roman Soldiers:

Yes, we're ready for a fight,
Yes, we're ready for a fight,
Yes, we're ready for a fight,
We're the Roman Soldiers.
or
Yes, we'll have a war with you,
Yes, we'll have a war with you,
Yes, we'll have a war with you,
We're the Roman Soldiers.

Irish Soldiers:

Shoot! Bang! Fire!

113

ALL IN! ALL IN!

Roman Soldiers:

    Now we've only got one leg,
    Now we've only got one leg,
    Now we've only got one leg,
    We're the Roman Soldiers.

(Appropriate actions accompany each attack until they are down dead).

Irish Soldiers:

    Shoot! Bang! Fire!

Roman Soldiers:

    Now we've only got one eye,
    Now we've only got one eye,
    Now we've only got one eye,
    We're the Roman Soldiers.

Irish Soldiers:

    Shoot! Bang! Fire!

Roman Soldiers:

    Now we've only got one arm,
    Now we've only got one arm,
    Now we've only got one arm,
    We're the Roman Soldiers.

Irish Soldiers:

    Shoot! Bang! Fire!

Roman Soldiers:

    Now we've got no arms at all,
    Now we've got no arms at all,
    Now we've got no arms at all,
    We're the Roman Soldiers.

Irish Soldiers:

    Shoot! Bang! Fire!

Roman Soldiers:

> Now we're dead and in our graves,
> Now we're dead and in our graves,
> Now we're dead and in our graves,
> We're the Roman Soldiers.

Irish Soldiers:

> Shoot! Bang! Fire!

Roman Soldiers:

> Now we're all alive again,
> Ready to fight and die again,
> Now we're all alive again,
> We're the Roman Soldiers.

Then the game starts all over again with the 'Irish' dying and coming to life again.

ALL AROUND THE VILLAGE

One child goes around the inside of the circle while they all chant the verse:

> All around the village,
> All around the village,
> All around the village,
> As we have done before.
> Stand and face your partner,
> Stand and face your partner,
> Stand and face your partner,
> As you have done before.

For these lines she stands in front of the child she has reached at the end of the fourth line. Now they both weave in and out through the circle while they all chant:

> Follow her to Dublin,
> Follow her to Dublin,
> Follow her to Dublin,
> As you have done before.

ALL IN! ALL IN!

Then while dancing around together they all chant:

> Dance before you leave her,
> Dance before you leave her,
> Dance before you leave her,
> As you have done before.

Sometimes a group of children may just catch hands and skip along chanting the verses.

All Around the Village was very popular about ten years ago, it is not played very often nowadays.

I SENT A LETTER . . .

Any number can play. All the children sit in a circle with their hands behind their backs. Whoever is 'on it' goes around the outside of the circle and gives the 'letter' into someone's hands. Nobody else knows who has it because she actually pretends to give it to each one, as she comes to them. The 'letter' may be a small stone, or a hankie or a piece of paper. During this part of the game the following four lines are sung:

> I sent a letter to my love,
>
> And on the way I dropped it.
>
> Some of you have picked it up,
>
> And put it in your pockets.

116

Then she comes into the centre of the circle and pointing to different children says:

> It wasn't you,
> It wasn't you,
> It wasn't you,
> But it was ... *you!*

This child stands up and she is asked:
> Give me a loan of your fiddle,

to which she replies:
> There's a great big hole in the middle.

Then she is asked:
> Give me a loan of your pan,

to which she replies:
> Follow me around *that* way as fast as you can.

She indicates from which direction she is to be followed. She is chased in and out through the circle until she is caught and the 'letter' recovered.

WALLFLOWERS, WALLFLOWERS

The children hold hands and form a circle then move around singing the verse. The youngest child is named and must turn her back to the others though remaining part of the circle for the rest of the game. The verse is then repeated and the next youngest child is named and she turns her back to the game. The verse is repeated until the whole circle has been turned around.

> Wallflowers, wallflowers,
> Growing up so high,
> We're all pretty fair maids,
> Who would not like to die.
> Especially (*Name*),
> She is the youngest child,
> Oh fie for shame! Oh fie for shame!

So turn your back against the game.
Turn your back to salty Jack,
And say no more to me,
For if you do, I'll chop you up in two,
And that will be the end of you.
(*or* And that's the end of me and you).

Wall — flowers wall — flowers growing up so high, we're
all pretty fair maids who would not like to die. Es —
— pecially Ma–ry Mur —— phy, she is the youngest child. Oh
fie for shame! Oh fie for shame! So turn your back a — gainst the game. Oh
turn your back to Sal — ty Jack and say no more to me, for
if you do, I'll chop you up in two and that will be the end of you.

OLD ROGER IS DEAD

Having chosen 'Old Roger', 'An Old Apple Tree' and 'An Old
Woman', the rest of the children hold hands and form a circle. Then,
while they move around singing the verse, 'Old Roger' sits in the
centre of the circle. At the beginning of the second verse the child
chosen to be the 'Old Apple Tree' comes into the circle and stands
over 'Old Roger' waving her arms up and down imitating the
branches of a tree. At the fourth verse the 'Old Woman' comes

118

picking up the apples. The child chosen for this part takes up the hem of her dress with her left hand and with her right hand, goes through the motions of picking up the apples and putting them into her skirt. It ends with the 'Old Woman' pretending to be lame and weaving in and out of the circle with 'Old Roger' in pursuit.

Old Roger is dead and he lies in his grave, lies in his grave, lies in his grave. Old Roger is dead and he lies in his grave, ee — eye, lies in his grave.

Old Roger is dead and he lies in his grave,
Lies in his grave, lies in his grave.
Old Roger is dead and he lies in his grave,
Ee eye, lies in his grave.

There grew an old apple tree over his head,
Over his head, over his head.
There grew an old apple tree over his head,
Ee eye, over his head.

The apples got ripe and they fell to the ground,
Fell to the ground, fell to the ground.
The apples got ripe and they fell to the ground,
Ee eye, fell to the ground.

There came an old woman a-picking them up,
Picking them up, picking them up.
There came an old woman a-picking them up,
Ee eye, picking them up.

Old Roger got up and he gave her a clout,
Gave her a clout, gave her a clout.

119

Old Roger got up and he gave her a clout,
Ee eye, gave her a clout.

This made the old woman go hippety hop,
Hippety hop, hippety hop.
This made the old woman go hippety hop,
Ee eye, hippety hop.

IN AND OUT THROUGH THE DARKIE BLUEBELLS

The children form a circle. They join hands and hold them up so that
whoever is 'on it' can weave in and out underneath while all sing the
verse:

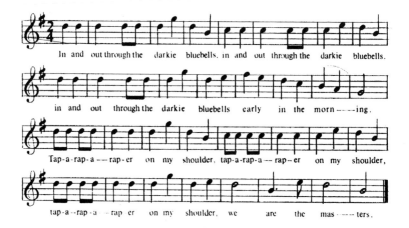

In and out through the darkie bluebells, in and out through the darkie bluebells,
in and out through the darkie bluebells early in the morn----ing.
Tap-a-rap-a---rap-er on my shoulder, tap-a-rap-a--rap-er on my shoulder,
tap-a--rap-a--rap-er on my shoulder, we are the mas----ters.

In and out through the darkie bluebells,
In and out through the darkie bluebells,
In and out through the darkie bluebells,
Early in the morning.

She stands behind whoever she has reached at the word 'morning'
and placing a hand on each shoulder she taps lightly while all sing:

32. Jackstones (p. 39)

33. Very young children are specially cherished (p. 4)

34. Picking sides (p. 48)

Tap-a-rap-a-rap-er on my shoulder,
Tap-a-rap-a-rap-er on my shoulder,
Tap-a-rap-a-rap-er on my shoulder,
We are the masters.

That child then goes behind the leader and catching her round the waist follows her round while all sing:

Follow me to the dear old Dublin,
Follow me to the dear old Dublin,
Follow me to the dear old Dublin,
Early in the morning.

The pattern is then repeated with another child added on each time until one big chain is formed instead of the circle. They start to run round fast in a circle until the chain breaks and it all ends in confusion.

LAZY MARY

'Lazy Mary' sits in the centre of the ring while the other children holding hands walk around singing:

Lazy Mary, will you get up,
Will you get up, will you get up.
Lazy Mary, will you get up,
On a cold and frosty morning.

121

Mary replies:

No, mother, I won't get up,
Won't get up, won't get up.
No, mother, I won't get up,
On a cold and frosty morning.

All sing:

If I give you a rasher and egg,
A rasher and egg, a rasher and egg.
If I give you a rasher and egg,
On a cold and frosty morning.

Mary replies:

No, mother, I won't get up,
Won't get up, won't get up.
No, mother, I won't get up,
On a cold and frosty morning.

All sing:

If I give you a doll and pram,
A doll and pram, a doll and pram.
If I give you a doll and pram,
On a cold and frosty morning.

Mary replies:

No, mother, I won't get up,
Won't get up, won't get up.
No, mother, I won't get up,
On a cold and frosty morning.

All sing:

If I give you a belt (*or* a whack) of the cane,
A belt of the cane, a belt of the cane.
If I give you a belt of the cane,
On a cold and frosty morning.

Mary replies:

Yes, mother, I will get up,
Will get up, will get up.
Yes, mother, I will get up,
On a cold and frosty morning.

'Mary' joins the circle and another takes her place in the centre.

The next three games became popular about five years ago.

OOSHA MARY MURPHY

The children stand in a ring while another child runs in and out through the ring. They all chant the verse:

> Oosha Mary Murphy,
> Oosha Mary Anne.
> Oosha Mary Murphy,
> And grab your partner's hand.

At the last line she takes the hand of one of the children in the ring and draws her into the centre of the ring, swings around with her and then leaves her to be 'Mary Murphy' while she herself goes back in the ring.

LITTLE MARY

'Little Mary' sits in the centre of the circle, while the other children holding hands move around chanting:

> Little Mary in her tent,
> And nobody comes to see her,
> But a little mouse.
> Rise Mary!
> Close your eyes!
> Point to the east,
> Point to the west,
> Point to the little girl
> That you like the best.

At 'Rise Mary' 'Mary' stands up, closes her eyes, points to the east and to the west, then picks the girl she likes best who then becomes 'Mary' and the game starts all over again.

DEAR ANNE

This is similar to *Little Mary*, but in this case 'Anne' stands in the centre of the ring while they go around saying:

> Dear Anne, dear Anne,
> You're only sixteen.
> Your father's a farmer,

123

And you are the queen.

Put your hands on your hips,
   (At this they all put their hands on their hips)

And a haw, haw, haw, haw,

And a haw, haw, haw, haw.

Dear Anne, dear Anne,

Come dancing with me.

Now they stop going around and stand with hands out-stretched towards 'Anne'. She picks one by tipping the hands of the chosen one upwards. 'Anne' goes back into the ring while the child chosen is 'Anne' for the next game.

THERE WAS A GIRL IN OUR SCHOOL.

Any number can play. All stand in a circle and at the words 'this is the way she went' they are free to perform any miming actions they think fit. The children's love of mimicry and caricature gets full rein in this and the next two games.

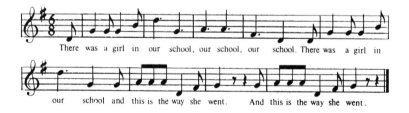

There was a girl in our school, (in) our school,
   (in) our school.

There was a girl in our school,

And this is the way she went.

And this is the way she went.
   (Actions)

Then she became a lady, a lady, a lady.
Then she became a lady,
And this is the way she went.
And this is the way she went.
  (Actions)

Then she became a teacher, a teacher, a teacher.
Then she became a teacher,
And this is the way she went.
And this is the way she went.
  (Actions)

Then she got married, married, married.
Then she got married,
And this is the way she went.
And this is the way she went.
  (Actions)

Then she had a baby, a baby, a baby.
Then she had a baby,
And this is the way she went.
And this is the way she went.
  (Actions)

Then the baby died, died, died.
Then the baby died,
And this is the way she went.
And this is the way she went.
  (Actions)

Then she got a donkey, a donkey, a donkey.
Then she got a donkey,
And this is the way she went.
And this is the way she went.
  (Actions)

Then the donkey kicked her, kicked her, kicked her.
Then the donkey kicked her,
And this is the way she went.
And this is the way she went.
  (Actions)

Then the lady died, died, died.
Then the lady died,
And this is the way she went.
And this is the way she went.
(Actions)

WHEN I WAS A . . .

Anyone in the circle is free to name anyone they think will lend
themselves to good miming, there is no limit to the possibilities.

When I was a wash'woman, a wash'woman, a wash'woman, when
I was a wash'woman, a wash'woman was I. I went
this way, I went that way, I went this way, I went that way. When
I was a wash'woman, a wash'woman was I.

When I was a washerwoman,[1] a washerwoman,
  a washerwoman,
When I was a washerwoman, a washerwoman was I.
      (Actions)
I went this way, I went that way,
I went this way, I went that way.
When I was a washerwoman, a washerwoman was I.

When I was a soldier, a soldier, a soldier,
When I was a soldier, a soldier was I.
      (Actions)

[1] Pronounced *washwoman*.

126

I went this way, I went that way,
I went this way, I went that way.
When I was a soldier, a soldier was I.

When I was a sailor, a sailor, a sailor,
When I was a sailor, a sailor was I.
(Actions)
I went this way, I went that way,
I went this way, I went that way.
When I was a sailor, a sailor was I.

When I was a policeman, a policeman, a policeman,
When I was a policeman, a policeman was I.
(Actions)
I went this way, I went that way,
I went this way, I went that way.
When I was a policeman, a policeman was I.

THE DUMMY'S BAND

This piece of mime causes more laughter than any other game. The more players you have the better for the band. The leader or in this case the 'conductor' whispers the name of a musical instrument into the ear of each child so you don't know until the 'conductor' gives the signal to start what instrument is on either side of you. You must play your instrument in absolute silence, whoever laughs is 'out'. But you can imagine what happens when the trombone player starts to hit the head of the player in front or the enthusiastic pianist encroaches upon the violinist next to him.

THE WEE POLONY MAN

The Dummy's Band is also the basis for another game sometimes played indoors and called *The Wee Polony Man*. The 'conductor' chooses an instrument for himself other than what the other players have been given, say, a melodeon. When they have mimed the instruments for a few minutes he says the verse.

I'm the wee Polony man.
I do everything I can,
To catch the wee Polony man.

All the other players must watch him carefully because at the end of the verse he changes instruments and starts to mime, say, the fiddle. So the player who was miming the fiddle must instantly start miming the melodeon. Any player who fails to change over on time is out.

A simpler version is played as follows: All the players mime whatever instrument the leader decides on and each time he recites the verse they must all change over to whatever new instrument he decides on. *The Dummy's Band* and *The Wee Polony Man* were originally played as 'funeral games' during a wake. But since wakes in Dublin are no longer the social occasions they once were, these games have lost some popularity.

DANCING UP THE HIGHWAY

Any form of dance that takes the children's fancy can be executed while singing this verse:

Dancing up the highway,
Dancing down the low way,
There I met a pretty maid,
Dancing gaily back again.
Fair maid, pretty maid,
Will you marry me,
And I'll take you back
To my own country.

They may just link their arms and skip backwards and forwards or they may do something more elaborate by forming sets of four, each two facing each other. Then they sing the verse dancing a sort of reel (nothing formal) towards each other and away again and when they reach the line:

Fair maid pretty maid,

they stop and face each other until the last line is reached and then they start dancing again.
This piece of entertainment was popular up to about ten years ago.

From Kerb to Kerb

No man-made toy, however ingenious, could offer as much pleasure to a child on a fine summer's day as a game of *Evens and Odds* or *Traffic Lights*. These games are simplicity itself. A leader is chosen and is always called 'Man' whether it's a boy or a girl. The 'Man' stands on one kerb while all the others stand on the opposite one and try to get across. Before long, every small child knows the even numbers from the odd ones, and in no time at all they learn what the colours of the traffic lights signify.

EVENS AND ODDS

Any number can play. A 'Man' is picked to call out the numbers. It's a very simple game but causes great excitement because it's both a physical and a mental exercise. The children line up on the kerb at one side of the road. The 'Man' decides whether they're to run for, even numbers or odd numbers. If 'Odds' are decided upon, they all run to the opposite kerb when he calls an odd number, and they remain where they are for the 'Evens'. Usually a lot of 'Odds' are called in rapid succession then suddenly an even number is called. Those who move are 'out'. The last one left, wins the game, and it's his chance to be 'Man' for the next game.

TRAFFIC LIGHTS

This is a variation on the game above. The 'Man' calls out the colours of the traffic lights. For *orange* and *green* all run from one kerb to the opposite and back again and continue with this until *red* is called when all must come to an immediate halt. Whoever fails to stop takes over at calling out the colours.

BREAD AND WATER

This is a further variation of the two previous games. In this one the 'Man' calls out all sorts of eatables beginning with 'Bread and Water' and continuing with any other more delectable things he can think of. At the mention of these all run to the opposite kerb, but at the mention of something like 'the leg of a chair' or anything else not eatable all must stay put. Whoever is caught moving is 'out'. The last one left in, wins the game, and is 'Man' for the next game.

COCK-COCK-A-ROOSHY

'Johnny' stands on one kerb while all the others stand on the opposite one, and perform the various actions as they occur.

All together call out:	Johnny may I go across the water?
Johnny:	*No* to-day but *Yes* to-morrow.
All:	Is the water deep?
Johnny:	Put down your finger and see.
All:	Oh! Johnny I lost my golden ring!
Johnny:	Put down your head and see.
All: ‹	Oh! Johnny I lost my golden crown!
Johnny:	Put down your foot and see.
All:	Oh! Johnny I lost my golden slipper!
Johnny:	Cock-cock-a-rooshy!

The first in the row then hops across on one foot with arms folded. 'Johnny' hops across the same way and tries to prevent her getting past him. If he succeeds he has another chance at being 'Johnny'. If she manages to get past him and reach the opposite kerb, still hopping on one foot, and arms still folded, she is 'Johnny' for the next game.

JOHNNY MAY I GO ACROSS THE WATER?

Any number can play: the children are divided into two sides. One side represents the waves and stands on the kerb opposite the other side whose aim is to cross the water against the waves.
'Johnny' stands at the side.
They call out together:

Johnny may I go across the water?

If 'Johnny' answers:

No today but *Yes* to-morrow,

nobody moves; but if he answers:

Yes to-day and *No* to-morrow,

they go on to ask:

Is the water deep?

'Johnny' replies:

Put down your foot and see.

At this they all try to hop across on one foot with their arms folded in front. The 'waves' in like manner set out to obstruct them. Whichever side has the most 'men' left on reaching the opposite bank wins, but it usually collapses in laughter half way across.

GIANT STEPS

Any number can play. All the children line up on one kerb. The idea is to get across to the opposite kerb as soon as possible. The 'Man' standing on the opposite kerb gives a command to each one in turn.

Take two baby steps!	Two tiny steps are taken.
Take one giant step!	One long step is taken.
Take one scissors!	A scissors-like step is made.
Take one spit in the bucket!	You spit forward and then jump that far.

132

Take one umbrella!	You twirl around moving forward at the same time.
Take a head of cabbage!	You take one jump forward.

You might think you are doing very well until you're told to
Take a rotten egg!

At this you must go right back to the start, but this command usually causes such a row that it is seldom given. Whoever is first across wins and is the 'Man' for the next game.

UNCLES AND AUNTS

I suppose this game could more accurately be called *Giant Steps* because only giant steps are taken. The 'Man' stands on the opposite kerb as before, but this time he calls out various Uncles, and Aunts. If he calls 'Uncle Joe', any child having such an uncle takes a giant step. Likewise if he calls 'Aunt Nora' any child having an aunt of that name takes a giant step. The child who reaches the opposite kerb first is 'Man' for the next game. A game like this lends itself to cheating, but in fact, nobody ever cheats because since they all know each others' relatives, a pretended uncle or aunt would be quickly detected.

SALLY-O

Any number can play. The 'Man' twirls around at varying degrees of speed saying:

Sally-o, Sally-o, one, two, three.

The others all move forward while he is twirling but they must be at a standstill when he stops at *three*. If one is caught while moving she must go back to the start. Whoever gets to the opposite kerb first wins and takes her turn at being 'Man'.

Good v. Evil

STATUES

The children stand in a line. The 'Man' takes each child by the hand and pulls her out sharply. She must remain statue-like in whatever position she is in when she comes to a halt. Each tries to land in the funniest position. Then the 'Man' tickles each one under the chin to try and make her laugh. Those who laugh go to 'Hell' and those who do not, go to 'Heaven'. I'm afraid most of them go to 'Hell'.

To make it more amusing, when each one has taken up a funny position, the 'Man' goes around each one again and offers a choice of items asking:

> What would you like? *A plate, a pinch, a stamp, a tickle, a funny face.*

Each gets whichever she chooses as follows:

A plate: 'Man' claps his hands together near her eyes but she must not blink.

A pinch: She gets a pinch and she must bear it without complaint.

A stamp: She gets a stamp on the foot.

A tickle: She is tickled but she must not laugh.

A funny face: 'Man' makes funny faces but she must not laugh.

Remembering the funny positions already taken up by each child, you can imagine what a hilarious game this can be.

134

MONDAY, TUESDAY

Seven children are each given the name of a day of the week. Another three are called the 'Maid', the 'Mother' and the 'Beggar'.

The 'Maid' is left minding the children while the 'Mother' goes to town. The 'Beggar' knocks at the door and asks the 'Maid' for bread. When she goes off to get the bread the 'Beggar' grabs 'Monday'. The 'Mother' comes back and asks where 'Monday' is. The 'Maid' gives all sorts of excuses, she can be as inventive as she likes: *Gone to pick flowers; Gone to buy a new hat; Gone to the well for water.*

The 'Mother' accepts this and goes off to town again. The 'Beggar' comes again and asks for milk. The 'Maid' goes off to get it and he grabs 'Tuesday'. When the 'Mother' returns and asks for 'Tuesday' she is told: *She is gone to find Monday.* The pattern is repeated with the 'Beggar' asking for a different thing each time he calls, until all the children are gone. The 'Mother' then goes to the 'Beggar's' house and demands the children back. The game ends with a general scramble for possession of the children.

I'M STIRRING MY CHICKEN (I)

This is a variation on the previous game. The 'Maid' is left to look after the 'Chicken' which is cooking in the pot. Usually the smallest child is chosen as the 'Chicken'. The 'Maid' sings:

> I'm stirring my chicken, my chicken, my chicken,
> I'm stirring my chicken till the master comes home.

The 'Beggar' comes to the door and asks for something and while she is gone to get it he steals the 'Chicken'. When the 'Maid' returns and finds the 'Chicken' gone, she puts another one in its place and continues to sing the verse until the 'Beggar' knocks again. The pattern is repeated until all the 'Chickens' are gone and the 'Master' comes home. When he discovers the 'Chickens' are gone he goes to the 'Beggar' and demands the 'Chickens' back. There is a general scramble for possession of the 'Chickens'.

I'M STIRRING MY CHICKEN (II)

Eleven children, boys and girls, are needed for this game. They each play the following parts:

> Seven 'Chickens' named Monday to Sunday:
> The 'Maid' minding them:
> The 'Master' at work:
> The 'Robber' who steals the chickens:
> The 'Butcher' who buys them from him.

The 'Maid' is stirring a 'Chicken' in the pot, singing:

> I'm stirring my chicken, my chicken, my chicken,
> I'm stirring my chicken till the master comes home.

The 'Robber' knocks at the door and the 'Maid' opens it. He demands bread, she says she has none. He then says *I'll spit on your floor!* She says *I dare you!* He spits on the floor and when she makes to put him out he says *Your kettle is boiling over!* She turns to the kettle and he grabs 'Monday'. The 'Maid' then puts another 'Chicken', 'Tuesday', into the pot and is singing *I'm stirring my chicken ...* when the 'Master' comes in and counts the 'Chickens' and asks *Where's Monday?* The 'Maid' replies *He's gone for an ounce of wool, he won't be long.*
The pattern is repeated until all the 'Chickens' are gone. Then the 'Master' and the 'Maid' go to the 'Butchers' for more 'Chickens'. The 'Maid' asks *Have you a nice fat chicken for sale?* The 'Butcher' says he has, and taking 'Monday's' leg he shows it to her with great praise *for this fine fat chicken.* But the 'Master' says *That's Monday!* and grabs her back. The pattern is repeated until all the 'Chickens' are restored to the 'Master'. Then the 'Robber' comes back and there's a general scuffle as the 'Butcher' and the 'Robber' try to gain possession of the 'Chickens' from the 'Maid' and the 'Master'.

GHOST IN THE GARDEN

The 'Mother' sends one of the 'Children' down the garden to get the clothes from the line. The 'Child' goes down the garden and the 'Ghost' frightens her away. She runs back to the 'Mother' crying *There's a ghost in the garden!* but the 'Mother' says *There's no ghost in the garden, it's only a head of cabbage.* So she gives her a few slaps and sends her up to bed. The next 'Child' is sent to get the clothes but with the same result. When the last 'Child' comes back the 'Mother' decides there must be something amiss so she brings all the 'Children' with her down the garden and they meet the 'Ghost'.

Mother: What do you want here?
Ghost: I want a needle and thread.
Mother: What's the needle and thread for?
Ghost: To sew my bag.
Mother: What do you want to sew the bag for?
Ghost: To carry sand.
Mother: What do you want the sand for?
Ghost: To sharpen my knife.
Mother: What do you want the knife for?
Ghost: To cut your throats!

At this they all run screaming away with the 'Ghost' chasing them. If he catches one of them he pretends to cut her throat with his hand. Then this 'Child' is 'Ghost' for the next game and the 'Ghost' is the 'Mother' for the next game.

GOOD ANGEL, BAD ANGEL

A 'Man', a 'Good Angel', and a 'Bad Angel', are chosen. The rest of the children stand in a row, the 'Angels' stand one on either side of the row and a little away from it. The 'Man' whispers a different colour in each child's ear. Then he calls out:

> Good angel, good angel,
> Fly with your wings.

The 'Angel' 'flies' over and taking a lock of the 'Man's hair, pulls it gently saying: Ding, dong, dell.
Man: What do you want today?
Good Angel: I want a box of colours.
Man: What colour?
Good Angel: Red.

If this is a 'wrong' colour, that is to say, nobody has been given it, they call out:

> Go home and wash your red face!

137

But if a child has the colour she goes over to the 'Good Angel'. Now 'Man' calls out:

> Bad angel, bad angel,
> Fly with your wings,

and the game proceeds as for the 'Good Angel' until there are two sides and the game ends with a tug of war.[1]

COLOURS

The 'Man' whispers a different colour in each child's ear. The 'Devil' comes to the door and asks for a colour. If one of the children has been given this colour she is called out. The 'Man' counts three and the child must run to a certain spot that is called 'Heaven'. If she gets there without the 'Devil' catching her she stays there. If not she must go to 'Hell' with the 'Devil'. It ends with a tug of war[1] between 'Hell' and 'Heaven'.

[1] Each angel lines his side up behind him, each child placing his hands around the waist of the child in front. The angels then take each others' hands and each side pulls as hard as possible, each trying to draw the other over an agreed line. It ends in great confusion and laughter.

Strength

RED ROVER

Two sides of equal number face each other. The side with first call names a child on the opposite side saying:

Red rover, red rover, I call (*Name*) over.

They start to count up to ten and the child called, then tries to break through the other side. If he succeeds he takes one of that side back to his own side with him. If he fails he is captured by that side. The game can go on indefinitely.

HALF OF THE CASTLE

This game can be played as a game on its own or as a preliminary to *Here's the Robbers Passing By*. (It also has the same air).
Two children form *Half of the Castle* by standing facing each other. One holding up her right hand takes the other child's left hand and this incomplete 'arch' is *Half of the Castle*. All the other children form a single line one behind the other, each holding on to the 'tail' (the hem of the coat or dress) of the child in front. In this way they go under the *Half of the Castle* already built singing:

Half of the castle is built, built, built.
Half of the castle is built,
My fair lady.

Then the two put up both hands to complete the 'castle' and the other children go through singing:

All of the castle is built, built, built.
All of the castle is built,
My fair lady.

From this they usually go on to play *Here's the Robbers Passing By*. Up to about six years ago *Here's the Robbers* ... had no such introduction.

HERE'S THE ROBBERS PASSING BY

This game is really an elaborate prelude to a tug of war game. First of all two children are picked to be 'on it'. These two each think of something especially nice with which to tempt the others to their side. One may choose *an apple and a pear,* the other *ice-cream and chocolate.* Having decided on this they form an 'arch' with their raised hands and the others pass under in single file singing:

Here's the robbers passing by,
Passing by, passing by.
Here's the robbers passing by,
My fair lady.

What did the robbers do to you,
Do to you, do to you.
What did the robbers do to you,
My fair lady.

Stole my watch and stole my chain,
In Bow Lane, in Bow Lane.
Stole my watch and stole my chain,
My fair lady.

Here's the robbers passing by, passing by, passing by

Here's the robbers passing by, my fair la —————— dy

What did the robbers do to you, do to you, do to you

What did the robbers do to you, my fair la —————— dy

Stole my watch and stole my chain, in Bow Lane, in Bow Lane.

Stole my watch and stole my chain my fair la —————— dy.

CHIP, CHOP, THE LAST MAN'S HEAD CUT STRAIGHT CLEAN OFF.

At the last line each child gets a separate word and the 'arch' is brought down on each head like a guillotine as it passes under. Whoever is reached at *off* is brought a little distance away and given a choice of something nice. She goes behind the one whose thing she chooses. The pattern is repeated until each child is on one side or the other. Then a tug of war[1] takes place.

[1] See footnote on p. 138.

141

Guessing Games

TOWNS AND COUNTIES

Any number can play. Indeed even two children can amuse themselves playing it. When it's played on the street the children are divided into two sides. One side decides on the name of a town or county. Then they invent a story which includes the various syllables of the place chosen. The other side must guess the name of the place. One of the most familiar ones is:

Wicklow: (always used to make newcomers familiar with the game):
   "One dark Winter's night a little girl had to visit her grandmother, there were no lights on the road so she took a paraffin-oil lamp with her. She put a new *wick* in before she set out. She couldn't open the gate when she got to her grandmother's house but the railing was *low* and she was able to climb over".

All sorts of miming actions can then be done to give clues, but all the fun is in the inventing of the story.

O'CLOCK

For this game two are picked to be 'on it' – and one of them is chosen for 'Man'. All the other children stand in a row. The two go a little distance away and the 'Man' decides on a certain time, say, half past eight. He whispers this to the other child who then comes

142

before the others and asks them to guess *What o'clock is it*? The child who guesses the correct time chases the 'Man' and if he catches him he brings him back to the line of children and he himself then becomes 'Man' and chooses the next *o'clock*. If he doesn't catch him he goes back to his place in the line.

WOOLWORTH'S

The children are divided into two sides. The side which is 'on it' decide among themselves on a certain thing that they have bought in Woolworth's, say a *Large Saucepan*. They then move over towards the other side saying:

As I went into Woolworth's, I bought an *L.S.*

The other side try to guess what the initials stand for. If they guess correctly, the first side turn and run back to their 'den' while the others try to catch one of them before they reach it. Whoever they catch must go over to the other side. The game goes on indefinitely with brains being racked and men lost and gained on both sides.

TELEVISION ADS

For this guessing game a 'Man' is chosen and the rest must guess what the initials of the television personalities or programmes, which he chooses, stand for. This game became popular with the advent of television.

Chasing

TIP AND TIG

This is one of the most impromptu and popular of all street-games.
Any number great or small can play and it usually serves to warm up
the children for other games. All that is required is for one child to
tip another saying *You're on it!* The child thus tipped has *tig* and
proceeds to chase the others. She tips another saying *Tig* and it's
then her turn to do the chasing. It can go on indefinitely. Any child
needing to be exempted from the game for a few minutes must
indicate this to whoever is 'on it' by raising the crossed index and
middle finger of one hand and calling *PAX!* ('Pax' can be asked for
in all chasing games.)

STICKY APPLE

This is the same as *Tip and Tig* but to add more fun and variety to
it, the child tipped must keep her hand on whatever part of her was
tipped until she gives *tig* to someone else. It's all right if she is tipped
on the head or shoulder but it's not so easy to run and try to tip
someone else when you have to hold your knee or your elbow!

DUCK CHASING

This is yet another variation of the previous games. When the child
who is doing the chasing is about to tip one of the other children,

that child *ducks* to avoid being tipped. If she doesn't *duck* in time she must do the chasing.

I'VE NO IRON

This is yet another version of *Tip and Tig*. Whoever is 'on it' chases the others who keep calling out *I've no iron!* to draw you after them. The idea is that if you are standing on, or holding, iron you are 'safe'. Usually you make for a railing or lamp-post or shore covering. Whoever is caught with 'no iron' must do the chasing.

FOLLOW THE ARROW

The children are divided into two sides. This is done in the following manner. The two senior children automatically assume the roles of leaders. Then the rest of the children form a line and the two leaders stand in front of them and alternately each one picks out a man for his side. As each child is called he stands behind his leader. But to decide who has first pick, one of the leaders turns away and wets the palm of one of his hands with a spit. Then he closes both fists, crosses them and holds them out to the other leader. If he picks the wet one he has first pick – or it may be decided that if he picks the dry one he wins. When the two sides have been chosen, with equal numbers on both sides (boys and girls), it is then decided which side will chase the other. This is also decided in the same manner as before.
The side that has first 'out', that is, the side to be chased by the other side, chalk a map of the area they will cover. Having decided on a certain destination in this area they decide on the route to be taken to it. Then they indicate this route half way with a series of arrows, the last arrow at a spot that could lead in several directions. The map is then shown to the leader of the other side who must count to a hundred (in fives) before giving chase, to give the first side a chance to get away. Each man on the pursuing side marks an opposite man on the other side and captures him. The pursuers must bring back their captives all together. This gives the boys and girls on each side a chance to pursue their favourites. This game is not played as formally as I have set it down. Many variations take place according to the mood of the moment. The whole thing often becomes a re-enactment of a film seen on television or in the cinema.

KICK THE CAN

Any number can play. All that is needed is an empty can. The 'Man' is chosen to guard the 'den'. He must cover his face while all the others go off and hide. He usually gives them up to one hundred to do this, counting out loud in fives: *Five, Ten, Fifteen,* etc. Then, if he thinks a child is in a certain hiding-place (e.g. a neighbour's garden) he takes the can, and banging it on the ground calls out the name of the child and the name of the family in whose garden he is hiding:

I spy John Healy in Murphy's garden, *one, two, three, come out!*

The can is left on the ground in the 'den', while the 'Man' keeps his eyes on the suspected hiding-place. If it's a 'right spy' the child named must come out, and go into the 'den' until he is 'relieved'. If it's a 'wrong spy' the child named, finding the 'Man's' attention diverted, leaves his actual hiding-place, and creeps up to the 'den' unknown to the 'Man' and when he gets the chance, kicks the can as far as he can calling out *Wrong spy!* The 'Man' must follow the can and while doing this whoever is in the den is 'relieved' and can go off and hide again.

RELIEVE-EE-O

The more players for this the better. They divide into two teams and a 'Man' is chosen to mind the 'den'. Then it's decided which team will chase and try to capture the other. When a child is captured he is brought back to the 'den'. He must stay there until he is 'relieved'. This is done if one of his own side succeeds in running through the 'den' shouting out *Relieve-ee-o!* All those who are in the 'den', thus relieved, run off again and rejoin their own side. Anyone caught by the 'Man' must remain in the 'den'. The game goes on until all the side is captured. Then it's the turn of those who were chased to do the chasing. During this game if there should be any dispute or if the game is to come to a temporary halt all those taking part are brought together by someone calling out repeatedly *All in, all in, the game is broke up!* This has the following very distinctive sound:

All in, all in! The game is broke up!

Another very distinctive sound is the air used by the boys as a rallying call: *Oo-ah Oo-ah all the gang!*

Oo — ah, Oo — ah, all the gang !

HIDE AND GO SEEK

The child who is to be 'on it' is decided by the following verse:

> Hide and go seek,
> The man in the beak.
> Who will be on it
> For hide and go seek.

The child reached at *seek* is 'on it'. He turns towards the wall or railings and covers his face so as not to see where the others go, and counts up to one hundred in fives to give them a chance to hide. Then to warn them he is coming to find them, he turns and calls out:

> Going, going,
> Ready or not.
> Keep your place
> Or you'll be caught.

If he suspects one is in a certain place he can sneak up and catch her and bring her to the 'den'. If he is almost certain a child is in a certain place, say behind a car, he can call out:

> I spy (*Name*)
> behind the red car
> 1, 2, 3, come out!

The child must then come out and wait in the 'den'. If, on the other hand she wasn't there she can come out of her hiding-place calling:

> Wrong spy eye o!

and she can go to another hiding-place. The game goes on until all are brought in.

WITCHES

One child is chosen to be the 'Witch' (a boy is better for this because there is a lot of chasing to be done). The 'Witch' stands apart from the others (in an 'orchard') with a length of rope in his hand, he is supposed to be asleep. The other children are supposed to be eating apples which they have stolen from the 'orchard'. To indicate this they make loud 'munching' sounds with their mouths. This munching wakens the 'Witch' who indicates he is rising up by stamping one foot on the ground. When the children hear this they run and the 'Witch' chases them. As he catches each child, he ties him in the rope and when they have all been caught he ties them securely to a lamp-post. Each child then tries to free himself and the last one free must be the 'Witch' for the next game.

CATCHING IN THE ROPE

Two 'Men' are picked to do the chasing. They carry a long rope between them. They usually give the others a short count—about fifty counted in fives, to get away. Then the chase begins. As each one is caught he is tied in the rope and the excitement mounts as the crowd in the rope increases.

COLOUR CHASING

Any number can play. The children stand close together in a circle. Each child puts forward her right foot. Whoever is 'Man' touches each foot saying:

> My shoe is black,
> Please change your other foot.

The child whose foot is reached at *foot* withdraws her right foot and puts forward her left foot.
The formula is repeated but the child whose foot is changed a second time is out of the game for the time being. The child who is last to change her foot a second time is now 'on it' for a game of chasing. But first of all she calls a colour, say, *Blue*. Each child must touch the colour blue to be 'safe', that is she can't be touched while she is touching the colour blue. This colour can be anywhere, on a hall-door, a cardigan, even a chalk-mark on the road. The child who fails to touch blue is chased and if she is caught before she reaches anything blue she is 'Man' for the next game.

MR. FOX

One child is chosen to be 'Mr. Fox'. He stands with his back to the others. They stand a distance away from him and call out:

> *Mr. Fox what time is it?*
> He replies: *One o'clock.*
> They come a little nearer and ask again:
> *Mr. Fox what time is it?*
> He replies: *Half past one.*

This continues for a while and they get bolder each time until they are almost up to him. Then they ask again:

> *Mr. Fox what time is it?*
> He replies: *Time for my dinner!*

and he turns and chases them. The one he catches then becomes 'Mr. Fox'.

OLD GRANNY GREY

These two rhymes are used to incite *Old Granny Grey* and *Old Daddy Aiken* to turn and give chase. They can also be said when hopping a ball.

Old Gran—ny Grey, let's go out to play. I
won't go near the wa——ter to hunt the ducks a——way. I
let the ba——by fall, o—ver the gar—den wall. My
mother came out, and gave me a clout, and knocked me o—ver a bottle of stout.

ALL IN! ALL IN!

Old Granny Grey,
Let's go out to play.
I (*or* We) won't go near the water,
To hunt the ducks away.
I let the baby fall,
Over the garden wall.
My mother came out,
And gave me a clout,
And knocked me over
A bottle of stout.

OLD DADDY AIKEN

Old Daddy Aiken,
Stole a bit of bacon,
Hid it in his overcoat
(*or* Put it up the chimney)
For fear it might be taken.

Marbles

Marbles are played with equal skill and enthusiasm by both boys and girls. They first appear around the end of January, and the season lasts for about three or four weeks.

A large chalk marble is called a *taw;* a steel one is called a *steeler* (this is in fact a ball-bearing and can usually be coaxed from motor-mechanics or railway-men). These are used as 'master' marbles during play and the standard size chalk or glass marbles are paid out if the game is *in the real*. If there are no stakes the game is *in the cod*.

TAW THE 'HOLE

Any number can play. This game is played on a hard clay surface in which a small hole has been made. A certain distance between the starting-point and the hole is agreed upon. Your aim is to be first to get your marble into the hole. If you hit one of the other marbles 'en route' during play you claim a marble from that player. If you get your marble within a finger-span of another player's marble you can try to *span* them (that is, bring them together) with your thumb and middle finger (they must hit off each other). If you succeed, you claim a marble. If you fail you pay a marble.

STICKING IN

This is played on the same principle as skittles. Each player places an agreed number of marbles in a row against a wall. Then each player in turn takes aim at them from a certain agreed distance. Each player keeps whatever number of marbles he dislodges. The player who wins the last remaining marble(s) has first aim in the next game.

FOLLOW

This is played along the channel. The first player throws his marble along, as far as he likes, calling out: *Follow all the way!* The next player follows, trying to score a 'hit' for which he is paid a marble. If he doesn't score a 'hit' his marble rests where it is and the next player follows trying also to score a 'hit'. Every time a player scores a 'hit' (that is, hits the other player's marble) he must get one from that player. If nobody scores a 'hit' at the first throw, it is again the turn of the first player who usually, at this stage, finds the other marbles within easier hitting-distance.

During the game, which can go on indefinitely, you'll hear the players calling out: *Lie all bars!* which means you must leave the marble wherever it stops even if it has been stopped by some obstacle.

FIVES

This is played like the game above except that the marbles are harder to win, and only two play at a time. Each time a player hits the other player's marble he scores five and does not gain a marble until he has scored one hundred or whatever multiple of five has been agreed on. This method is used when marbles are scarce on both sides.

Beds

In any area where there is a large population of children, you couldn't fail to notice the various geometrical designs which cover the pavements, nor could you fail to become aware of the sounds peculiar to playing *Beds*. The scraping sound of the pickey as it is aimed into a certain bed, followed by the very definite footfall of the child as she goes from bed to bed kicking the pickey before her. The number of boys to be seen playing *Beds* has increased considerably lately; a few years ago only the girls played *Beds*. There are roughly three types of beds: *Pickey Beds, Ball Beds,* and *Name Beds*. Each type can be played on the various geometric designs drawn on the footpath or roadway with chalk or plaster. It is an interesting thing to note that the numbers of the beds are always drawn very carefully and with double lines.

PICKEY BEDS

Pickey Beds is the game most frequently played. The beds are numbered 1-8 or 1-10 and bed number four or five is usually a 'rest' bed and marked accordingly. But first you must have a pickey which is made in the following way:
An empty shoe-polish or ointment tin makes an ideal pickey. The tin is filled with moist clay to give it weight and then the lid is stamped well down with the heel so that is won't open during play. A good pickey is as important to a child as a tool is to a tradesman. It becomes a cherished possession, it is kept in a safe place, and is seldom if ever lent to anyone else in case its 'charm' might diminish.

Any number can play. Whoever is first starts off by throwing the pickey into bed number one. Then, hopping on one foot, she kicks the pickey from bed to bed never letting down the other foot except in the 'rest' bed. If she completes the round without fault she is *for two* so she throws the pickey into bed number two and so on. If, when she throws the pickey, it misses the bed or touches a line or if her foot touches a line or she looses her balance or 'inches' towards the pickey she is 'out' and the next child gets her chance. If a child is *for three* say, when she is declared 'out', when her turn comes around again she is still *for three* when she resumes play. She may have to wait a while before her turn comes around again, depending on how many are playing. If, in the meantime, another child is declared 'out' at bed number three the first child will chant:

> Up to me, up to me, never get apast me!
> Two in the one bed never can agree!

When the ten beds have been won, that makes a game. But very often she must go through various other rituals to complete the game. For example, she may be required to hop around the beds three times, or she may have to go from bed to bed blindfolded, without touching a line. When going from bed to bed for this, one instinctively seems to stretch out one's hands and call out for re-assurance *Am I in it?* If her feet are clear of the lines she can proceed to the next bed, and so on until all ten have been completed.

BEDS

This phrase *Am I in it?* survives on into adult life. Grown ups who happen to find themselves groping in the dark or picking their steps, will say jokingly *Am I in it?* remembering how they used this phrase when playing beds. Another ritual is to go from bed to bed with the pickey balanced on her head. She must complete a round without letting the pickey fall. Having succeeded thus far, she then turns her back on the beds and throws the pickey over her shoulder. If it lands in one of the beds without touching a line she claims that bed as her own by writing her name on it. Nobody else may step in this bed which makes it hard for them to get around because they must hop right over it. She, on the other hand, may 'rest' in it on her way around for the next game.

NAME BEDS I

5	6	15	16
4	7	14	17
3	8	13	18
2	9	12	19
1	10	11	20

Throw the pickey into No. 1. Leave it there and hop from one square to the next, never touching a line, as far as No. 10. Then bend over and take up the pickey and hop around the remaining beds. If you complete this without fault you write your name in one of the beds and this becomes for you a 'rest' bed in which you can take a 'rest' on the way around. Other players must hop over these 'rest' beds. The player who gets the most beds wins.

NAME BEDS II

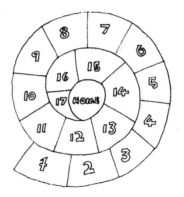

This is a variation on the ordinary square *Name Beds* and can be played with or without a pickey. A player must hop from square to square without a rest until she reaches the inner square which is 'home'. Then she makes the return journey and on completing this without error she gains a 'rest' bed and claims it by writing her name in it. As with the other beds nobody else may hop into this bed.

ROUNDY BEDS

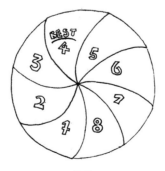

This is another variation of *Name Beds*. There are eight beds to be played with a 'rest' in bed number four.

After completing the eight beds she then starts the next round in reverse. She starts by being for eight, then seven, and right around until she has finished them all. She repeats the first bed once more. Having completed this she then chooses a bed for herself (other than number four) and writes her name in this bed. Nobody else may step in this bed which she uses as a 'rest' bed.

AEROPLANE BEDS

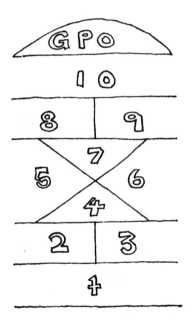

These beds may be played like ordinary *Pickey Beds*, hopping from bed to bed and 'resting' only in number ten before making the return journey. They may also be played in the following manner:

Throw the pickey into bed number one. Then leave it there and hop from bed to bed and back again and when you reach number one kick the pickey out. Then aim for bed number two, leave the pickey there and hop around as before until you reach number two on your way back. Then still on one foot and without 'inching' towards the pickey kick it into number one and then out. When you have completed the ten beds you may have to go through some of the other rituals before winning a game. You do not get a bed for yourself in these aeroplane beds.

Another variation is played as follows:
When the child has thrown the pickey into the bed, instead of hopping from bed to bed after that on one foot, she goes 'scissors' fashion along them, reaching number ten with her feet together. Then without resting, she twirls right around in number ten and comes back down in the same way. Then she can kick the pickey back from bed to bed as before, or, she can step forward on one foot, bend down and pick up the pickey, then hop back with it the rest of the way.

FRENCH BEDS

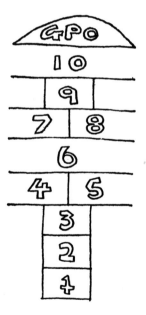

These are just a variant design of *Aeroplane Beds,* and they are played in the same way. More frequently, though, the pickey is picked up on the way back.

BALL BEDS

The path is chalked as for *Pickey Beds*.

You start by being *for one*, therefore you roll the ball into bed number one. Then, putting one foot into bed number one, you pick up the ball with one hand, hop it once, then once in each of the other beds, going from bed to bed with the ball hopping continuously (except in the 'rest' bed) and making sure that you only have one foot at a time in each bed and also making sure that you keep your feet clear of the lines at all times. When this is completed without fault you are *for two*. You roll the ball into bed number two. Then you step with one foot into bed number one and with the other foot into bed number two and bending down pick up the ball with one hand. Then hop the ball twice in bed number two and once in each of the other beds. When this is completed without fault you are *for three*. The first numbers are easy but the later ones more difficult. For example, when you're *for nine* it is difficult to go from bed to bed without fault in the short time it takes to roll the ball across from one to nine, because the ball must be caught within the bed. Of course being *for ten* is even more difficult.

Miscellaneous Games

SNAP THE BACON

Two teams of equal number stand facing each other. The 'Bacon' (usually a large stone) is placed in the centre between them. If there are twenty playing, with ten on each side, then each child gets a number from one to ten so that her opposite number is diagonally across from her. The 'Man' calls out: *Number one* (or *Number three,* etc.) *snap the bacon!* The two who are number one come over towards the 'Bacon'. The idea is to *snap the bacon* and get back to your place without being caught and gain one point for your side. If you are caught the other side gains the point. Whichever side gains most points wins. But before it can be snapped there is usually a very tense few minutes as each child bends towards the 'Bacon', with outstretched hand poised above it, each trying to decide whether he should have a try at snapping the 'Bacon' or concentrate on preventing the other one from getting away with it.

O'GRADY SAYS

Any number can play. 'O'Grady' stands facing the others and gives the commands:

O'Grady says – 'do this'

and 'this' can be anything like tipping your toes, marching, running, making funny faces, standing still, twirling around, etc. The commands are given very fast and are only obeyed when they are preceded by *O'Grady Says*. Anyone obeying when *O'Grady* is not mentioned is 'out'. The last man out wins the game and becomes 'O'Grady' for the next game.

THE CAT AND THE MOUSE

Two children are chosen, one to be the 'Mouse', the other to be the 'Cat'. All the others stand in a circle and they join hands and raise them up. The 'Mouse' stands in the centre of the ring and the 'Cat' stands outside it. The idea is to protect the 'Mouse' from the 'Cat' by preventing the 'Cat' from coming into the circle. The fun starts when the 'Mouse' teases the 'Cat' by venturing outside the circle and dashes back in again with the 'Cat' following close by and endeavouring to get in. If the 'Cat' catches the 'Mouse' the 'Cat' can then choose the next 'Mouse'.

PUSSY FOUR CORNERS

Five can play this. One (the 'Pussy') stands in the centre while the others stand one in each corner. They can change from one corner to the other by attracting the attention of the one into whose corner they want to get the same as you would call a cat *'Pish, wish, wish'*. If the 'Pussy' in the centre reaches one of the corners while it is vacant, whoever is displaced must go to the centre and be the 'Pussy'.

BALL BETWEEN THE FEET

Any number can play. The children are divided into two teams. The first child on each team has a ball. When told to 'go' each puts the ball between his feet and then they must jump to a certain point and back without losing the ball. If one loses the ball on the way he must start again. The team to finish first wins.

GRANNY WENT TO MARKET

This game is something like the one above but each child is given the name of a commodity that can be bought at the market, bread, butter, tea, sugar, etc. on one side and apples, oranges, pears, etc. on the other.
The 'Granny' calls out:

Granny went to market and bought *tea* and *pears*.

The two representing these commodities must run to a certain point and back to their places. The first back gains a point for that side. The side with most points wins.

Another version of this game is played as follows: Supposing there are twelve players, each three are given the name of the same commodity. Then 'Granny' calls out:

Granny went to market and bought *apples*.

The three who represent apples run to a certain point and back. The first back gets a chance to be 'Granny'.

THE BIG SHIP SAILS

The big ship sails through the alley alley o, the alley alley o. the alley alley o. The

big ship sails through the alley alley o, on the nine-teenth of No—vem-ber

> The big ship sails through the alley, alley o,
> The alley, alley o, the alley, alley o.
> The big ship sails through the alley, alley o,
> On the 19th of November.

The leader stands with a hand against the wall, or the railing, or a lamp-post. All the others form a line holding hands. The first in the line takes the leader's free hand. They all walk under the leader's arm several times until the whole lot are in a tight knot. Still standing in this knot they repeat the verse and at the words '19th of November' they all throw up their hands causing much confusion and laughter.

SEW, SEW, SEW

This is very like *The Big Ship Sails,* but this time while the children are getting themselves into a knot they chant:

Sew, sew, sew, sew, thread a needle.

The last child under, ties the knot by taking hold of the leader's hand and asking:

Does my little chickies like ice-cream?

All answer: 'Yum, yum', and bend both knees up and down. He continues asking them if they like various things like *fruit, cake, sweets* and each time they all bend up and down and answer 'Yum yum'.
When you remember that they are all in a tight knot you'll realise the great fun this affords. Then he asks:

Does my little chickies like the sting of a bee?

At this they all answer 'No, no, no', and they break up and run. He chases them and whoever he catches takes his place for the next game and he goes up to the front to be leader.

I SPY . . .

Any number can play. The children stand in a row and the 'Man' stands facing them.

Man: I spy.
Children: Who do you spy?
Man: A little girl with K in her eye.

She chooses the initial of one of the children in the row. That child comes out and takes one of the 'Man's' hands and they both hop around on one foot while they all say the verse:

> K is for Kathleen,
> Pretty little Kathleen,
> She should have a baby.
> Wrap her up in calico,
> Send her to the alley o.
> A-B my baby.
> My old grandad he is dead,
> With twenty four candles on his head.
> Five on his fingers,
> Five on his toes,

ALL IN! ALL IN!

My old grandad he is dead.
A-B-C-D-E-F-G-H-I-J-K—

The alphabet is recited until the child's initial is reached. If she has managed to stay on one foot all this time she is 'Man' for the next game.

DID YOU EVER

The children stand in a row and the 'Man' stands facing them:

Man: Did you ever?
Children: No I never
Man: See a nigger
Children: Nigger who?
Man: Nigger Tom
Children: Tom who?
Man: Tom Chase
Children: Chase who?
Man: Chase *(Name)*!

The 'Man' names one of the children in the line. She comes out and she and the 'Man' take each other's right hand and both hop around on one foot repeating the question and answers. If the child named is able to hop on one foot to the end she is 'Man' for the next game. About four years ago I heard this game for the first time.

HOP, HOP, TO THE BAKER'S SHOP

For this game either of the following verses may be used:

Hop, hop, to the bak-er's shop, and see how long it takes you. Your mother will say you were playing with the boys from the U. S. A.

Hop, hop, to the baker's shop,
And see how long it takes you.
Your mother will say
You were playing with the boys
From the U.S.A.

———◆———

Hop, hop, to the baker's shop,
And see how long it takes you.
When you get there,
You're mother will be there,
So don't dilly dally on the way.

One child is chosen to be 'Man' and all the others line up facing him with their hands outstretched, palms down. The 'Man' goes along tipping each hand downwards as he says the verse. The hand reached at the last word is tipped upwards (from the palm).
As the 'Man' does this he runs and the child whose hand has been tipped shouts: *Stop!* If the 'Man' doesn't stop instantly, he must go back and start all over again. When he does stop, the other child must hop around him on one foot saying the verse—(for this, all the others join in too). When she finishes the verse (still on one foot, or she's 'out') she stops and the 'Man' (who has remained standing still) stretches out a hand. She must be able to tip the 'Man's' hand without losing her balance. If she succeeds she is 'Man' for the next game. If she doesn't, she goes back to her place in the line.
I heard this game for the first time about seven years ago.

LONG OR SHORT

This is similar to *Hop Hop*. The 'Man' goes along the line of outstretched hands tipping each one as he says:

Long or short,
Long or short,
Which would you rather have,
Long or short?

Whoever is reached at *short* must decide on *long* or *short*. Two distances have already been decided on, one long and one short. So, whichever the child chooses, say, *short,* she runs that distance while the man must run the longer one. Whoever gets back to the starting point first, wins and is 'Man' for the next game.

DUBLIN, DERRY, CORK, KERRY

These four counties are usually quoted in the riddle:

> Dublin, Derry, Cork and Kerry
> Spell me that without a K.

The answer of course is THAT.

Another use for the names of these four counties is in the following game: The more players available the better. First a 'Man' is chosen. Then all the other children are divided into four groups, one group for each county. When each one is sure to which group she belongs and which corner of the road has been alloted to her county, the 'Man' turns his back while all the others mingle together and dance and jump about. The 'Man' sings, or if he happens to have a whistle, he 'plays' it. He stops suddenly, and while he turns around to face them, they all run to their special corner. The 'Man' then calls out:

> Kerry has a broken leg!

At this everyone in 'Kerry' hops around on one leg. Then he calls out:

> Derry is blind!

At this everyone in 'Derry' walks around with both hands over their eyes. The 'Man' is free to think up anything he likes for a county, and naturally he tries to think up antics which will cause the most confusion and laughter. If a county is pronounced *dead* they are out of the game.

Various Verses

If there is no game in progress the children may simply sit around and sing, or chant out nonsense rhymes. Some of the verses they sing have interesting associations.

THE WAXIES' DARGLE

It is doubtful if many of the children who chant this little verse know anything of its associations:

Says my old one to your old one, will you come to the Wax-ies' Dar—gle. Says your old one to my old one, sure I hav—en't got a far—del.

> Says my old one[1]
> To your old one,
> Will you come to the Waxies' Dargle.
> Says your old one
> To my old one,
> Sure I haven't got a fardel.

[1] *Old one* (pronounced *owl wan*) means wife, or mother.

In Dublin a cobbler is called a waxy because he uses wax-end for stitching. Up to about 1890 the waxies of Dublin held an annual gathering at Irishtown Green (near Ringsend). This gathering was called the Waxies' Dargle. Stalls were erected for the sale of cockles and other delicacies, concertinas provided the music for the reels and set-dances which enlivened the occasion. A very gay time was to be had, but like all such gatherings you needed money and a fardel,[1] even in those days, wouldn't go very far. This little verse is all that remains to commemorate the once famous Waxies' Dargle.

CHEER BOYS CHEER

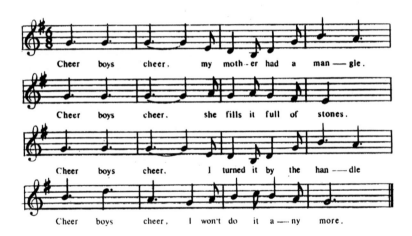

Cheer boys cheer. my moth-er had a man——gle.

Cheer boys cheer. she fills it full of stones.

Cheer boys cheer. I turned it by the han——dle

Cheer boys cheer. I won't do it a——ny more.

I have never seen a coffin-roller myself but this is what the old-fashioned mangle of fifty or sixty years ago was called in Dublin. It was an ungainly but very efficient affair, consisting of a large box-like wooden frame, for all the world like a coffin. The frame was propped on quantities of heavy stones against the impact of the four large rollers. The clothes were laid on the rollers which were operated by a huge handle placed mid-way on the frame. The rollers were first rolled in one direction along the whole length of the frame.

---

[1] *fardel* (Middle English =*fourth deal*) meaning a fourth part of anything. So a fardel in this case means a farthing.

Then they were rolled in reverse so that the mangled clothes came off the rollers and were folded and left ready for the customer.

Women made a living in those days by taking in mangling. There was at this time a row of cottages in Mary's Lane called 'Little Hell' and opposite this lived a woman who used to take in mangling, at 1½d. a dozen. Children loved to hang over the half door of her cottage to watch the operation of the coffin-roller.

All that remains to-day of this necessary and laborious work are the lines of this simple verse:

> Cheer boys cheer,
> My mother had a mangle.
> Cheer boys cheer,
> She fills it full of stones.
> Cheer boys cheer,
> I turned it by the handle.
> Cheer boys cheer,
> I won't do it any more.

DOWN IN THE ALLEY-O

Down in the al—ley—o, where we play rel-ieve-ee—o, up comes her mother—o,
Have you seen my Mary—o? She's down in the al—ley—o, kissing all the boys—o.

> Down in the alley-o,
> Where we play relieve-ee-o,
> Up comes her mother-o,
> Have you seen my Mary-o?
> She's down in the alley-o,
> Kissing all the boys-o.
> Oh! Oh! Mary-o,
> I wonder does your mother know?
> No! No! she doesn't know,
> She thinks I'm doing the washing-o.

I'VE A PAIN IN MY BELLY

'I've a pain in my belly'
Says Doctor Kelly.
'Rub it with oil'
Says Doctor Doyle.
'It's a very good cure'
Says Doctor Moore.
'It is in my hat'
Says Doctor Wyatt.

DOWN BY THE RIVER SAWL-YA

I know an old woman who lived in the woods,
Weel-ya, Weel-ya, Wall-ya.
I know an old woman who lived in the woods,
Down by the river Sawl-ya.

She had a baby three months old,
Weel-ya, Weel-ya, Wall-ya.
She had a baby three months old,
Down by the river Sawl-ya.

She had a penknife long and sharp,
Weel-ya, Weel-ya, Wall-ya.
She had a penknife long and sharp,
Down by the river Sawl-ya.

She stuck the knife in the baby's heart,
Weel-ya, Weel-ya, Wall-ya.
She stuck the knife in the baby's heart,
Down by the river Sawl-ya.

Three big knocks came to the door,
Weel-ya, Weel-ya, Wall-ya.
Three big knocks came to the door,
Down by the river Sawl-ya.

Two policemen and a man,
Weel-ya, Weel-ya, Wall-ya.
Two policemen and a man,
Down by the river Sawl-ya.

The policeman came to lock her up,
Weel-ya, Weel-ya, Wall-ya.
The policeman came to lock her up,
Down by the river Sawl-ya.

They put a rope around her neck,
Weel-ya, Weel-ya, Wall-ya.
They put a rope around her neck,
Down by the river Sawl-ya.

That was the end of the woman in the woods,
Weel-ya, Weel-ya, Wall-ya.
That was the end of the woman in the woods,
Down by the river Sawl-ya.

JANEY MAC

Janey Mac,
My shirt is black,
What'll I do for Sunday?
Go to bed,
And cover your head,
And don't get up
Till Monday.

I HAVE A GUMBOIL

I have a gum——boil, a tooth——ache, a bel—ly - ache, a pain in my left side, a pim—ple on my bum.

> I have a gumboil,
> A tooth-ache, a belly-ache,
> A pain in my left side,
> A pimple on my bum.

PRODDY WODDY ON THE WALL

> Proddy woddy on the wall,
> A half a loaf would feed you all,
> A ha'penny candle would show you light,
> To read your Bible in the night.

IF A GUMBOIL

> If a gumboil could boil oil,
> How much oil would a gumboil boil,
> If a gumboil could boil oil.

IF-IKA YOU-IKA

There's no fantasy or interest in a plain statement like:

> If you can swim like my son John
> I will give you a bob (*or* a shilling).

but with fancy endings added to give rhyme if not reason it becomes acceptable:

If-ika you-ika can-ika swim-ika[1]
Li-ika my-ika son-ika John-ika
I-ika will-ika give-ika you-ika
Bob-ika (*or* shilling[2]).

I SEE PARIS

I see Paris,
I see France,
I see a hole
In the Lord Mayor's pants.

It is usual to say 'I see Paris' to someone whose underwear is showing.

HOW IS YOUR OLD ONE

How is your old one? Game ball ! Out in the back-yard, playing ball.

How is your old one,[3]
Game ball.[4]
Out in the back-yard,
Playing ball.

---

[1] *i* as in *lick*.
[2] Pronounced *skilling* to alliterate with the -ika endings.
[3] *Old one* (pronounced *owl wan*) means wife, or mother.
[4] *Game ball* is a very common expression all over Dublin. If you ask someone how they are getting along they'll reply *game ball* which means: 'I'm not doing too badly; I'm doing very well'. It comes from the ball game of *hand-ball*: the last round to be played before a game is won is called: *game ball*.

OH! THE HORSE BROKE DOWN

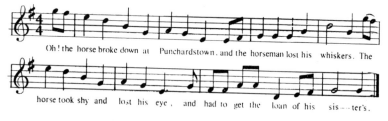

Oh! the horse broke down at Punchardstown. and the horseman lost his whiskers. The horse took shy and lost his eye, and had to get the loan of his sis — ter's.

Oh! the horse broke down
At Punchardstown,[1]
And the horseman lost his whiskers.
The horse took shy,
And lost his eye,
And had to get the loan of his sister's.

ROUND APPLE I

Round a — pple, round a — pple, as round as can be, for to see Mol — ly Byrne in her car — riage go round. In her car — riage, in her car — riage, 'by night and by day, she's driv — ing to see Paddy Rei — lly a — way.

[1]This is a mispronunciation of Punchestown (in County Kildare) where there is a famous race-course.

174

Round apple, round apple,
As round as can be,
(*or* And still we go round)
For to see (*Name*)
In her carriage go round.

In her carriage, in her carriage,
By night and by day.
She's driving to see
(*Name*)[1] away.

Then up comes her father,
With a knife in his hand,
Saying give me my daughter
Or your life I will have.

I care not, I care not,
I care not a pin,
For I love my (*Name*)
And my (*Name*) loves me.

ROUND APPLE (II)

Round apple, round apple,
How still it goes round,
For to see (*Name*)
In her carriage go round.

In her carriage, in her carriage,
By night and by day,
For to see (*Name*)[1]
With her always.

Out comes her dear mother,
With a knife in her hand,
Says give me my (*Name*)
Or your life I shall have.

I wash her in new milk,
And I dress her in silk,
And I write down her name,
With a gold pen and ink.

[1] The name of her sweetheart.

175

(*NAME*) SELLS FISH

> (*Name*) sells fish,
> Three ha'pence a dish.
> Cut the heads off,
> Cuts the tails off,
> (*Name*) sells fish.

CHEER UP...

In many parts of Dublin various roads have their own football team. There is tremendous rivalry between the teams and when one beats the other the winning team sings the following song in praise of themselves:

Cheer up 'Syc—a-more' they're known ev-ery—where. They knocked down 'Lib—er-ty' and left them ly—ing there. 'Liberty' called for mer——cy, but mer—cy was—n't there, so cheer up Syc—a-more they're known ev—ery——where. It's a rare old team to play for. It's a rare old team to know, for all we know there's going to be a fight, and good old 'Sycamore' will be there.

176

Cheer up 'Sycamore'
They're known everywhere.
They knocked down 'Liberty'
And left them lying there.
'Liberty' called for mercy,
But mercy wasn't there,
So cheer up 'Sycamore'
They're known everywhere,
It's a rare old team to play for,
It's a rare old team to know,
For all we know
There's going to be a fight
And good old 'Sycamore' will be there.
Lurry them up!
Kick their shins!
That's the way 'Sycamore' wins!

The last three lines are just chanted out.

—◆—

This is but a brief glimpse into the private world of the children in one very small area of Dublin. All the lore of this world is known to the parents (and grandparents) of the children – it was, after all, part of their childhood too, but it goes completely unnoticed by them now. A child coming home from school is often asked *What did you learn to-day? How did you get on at school to-day?* But nobody would ever think of asking a child coming in from play *How did you enjoy yourself? What games did you play?* But rather *Look at the cut of you! You'll have to be scrubbed before you go to bed!* And this is as it should be.

One of the most significant things about street-games is the fact that they are handed on by the children themselves to the younger ones. Unlike conventional nursery rhymes and fairy stories which are learned in the home, these street-games are learned and shared outside the home.

I have heard parents say that it is bad to give a child *the run of the street*. That is to say they fear that running free with other children may make a child 'common' or vulgar. But to deny a child this chance to enjoy the uninhibited freedom experienced in street-games is to impose a harsh and unnecessary restriction on the child. For it is only in these games that children are entirely free of adult supervision; and entirely free to come to terms unaided with their own generation. Here, each child is equally important because each one is necessary to the game. There is nobody to impress, there are no prizes to win, so there is little rivalry.

Setting down the games as I have done, gives them a certain formality which might be misleading. Seldom is a game played from start to finish without some interruption. Seldom does the craze for any particular game last more than a few days. It will be noticed that ready-made shop toys play no part in these street-games. The objects used, being simple, give full scope to the imagination and ingenuity of the child.

Since this is a private world there are many questions which must go unanswered. One wonders how suitable ropes seem readily available when swinging on a lamp-post, or skipping, is in vogue. Yet, no child has ever been known to buy a length of rope for the purpose, nor have I ever heard of anybody missing a clothes-line! Marbles appear as if by magic when they are required at the end of January. The same can be said of hoops. Do people suddenly find their bicycles minus a wheel in July? I've never heard it said. But as long as there are children to play on the street, ropes and marbles will appear in due season, as readily as jam-jars for catching bees and hoops for rolling.

The wealth and variety of the games being enjoyed by the children in this small area, will give some idea of the amount of children's traditional lore available, and as yet uncollected, throughout Ireland

CLASSIFIED INDEX

This index is an attempt to classify the subjects referred to in the games and speech of the children. It includes proper names, nicknames and refrains. The numbers refer to the pages. The word may occur more than once on a page.

Action-words (*words accompanied by certain actions*)
actions 86
alive again 115
all around 115
all in together 95, 96
alone-y 9
a–picking them up 119
archy 61, 64
baby steps 132
backy 61, 64
bang 113, 114, 115
basket 62
bow 86
buzz 34
by the hand 106
carry 34
catch 40, 42
chase 71, 164
chip, chop 141
chuck 70
claimy 62
clainy 62
clap clap 37
clap hands 5
clappy 62
close your eyes 123
clout 119, 120
clutch 42
cock-cock-a-rooshy 131
come along with me 106, 109
come back 81
come home 104
come in 81
crack 42, 102
cross-bars 85
cut straight clean off 141
dance 116; dancing 124, 129
dashy 61, 64
dead 115
ding dong dell 137
do this 160
down the hill 63
down the spout 88
downy 61, 64
duck 25, 144
eight pennies 87
eleven pennies 87

fingies 42
fire 113, 114, 115
first crack 38
five pennies 87
fly away 81
fly with your wings 137, 138
follow 115, 117, 121
four pennies 87
funny face 134
giant step 132
goes push 83
goffo 25
go for a long walk 104
good-bye 81
go round the moon 12
go to church 104
go up the stairs 84
grab your partner's hand 123
head of cabbage 133
hippety hop 120
hippy 62
hop 53
hop, hop, 165
hopping 154
I call for 78
in and out 120
in comes 80, 82, 83
in our graves 115
I went this way 126, 127
I went that way 126, 127
jelly-bag 62
jump(s) 96, 99
keep me up 35
kick them out 86
kicked (her) 125
kicks 85
kick the can 146
kneel down 104
left foot 53, 66
left leg 61, 64
leg and a duck 34
let me through 103
lies in his grave 119
like this 85
nine pennies 87
no arms at all 114
one arm 114
one eye 114

one leg 114
one penny 87
one step, two steps 6
'on it' 48, 49, 52, 70, 116, 120, 140,
    142, 143, 144, 145, 147, 148
oosha 9, 12, 123
open fingers 42
open the gates 103
open your mouth 22
out goes 50, 78, 83, 96
out walks 110
over 61, 64, 83
over the stars 99
over we go 55
over you go 54
passing by 140
peep through 88
pick 50, 102; – it up 86
pinch 134
plainy 61, 62, 64
plate 134
point to the east 123
point to the west 123
put down your finger and see 131
put down your foot and see 131, 132
put down your head and see 131
put on your ring 104
put out the light 84
put your hands on your hips 124
rainbow 63
reel 62
right foot 53, 62, 66
right leg 61, 64
ring-a-ring 12
rise Mary 123
rolley 62
rolling a hoop 46
rotten egg 133
round and round the garden 6
run around the corner 86
run into 70
run out of 70
run through 84
sails through 162
salute 86
say your prayers 84, 104
scissors 132
scram 81
scut(ting) 25
see-saw 7
seven pennies 87
sew, sew, sew sew 163
shake 34; – hands 6

shilling 87
shoot 113, 114, 115
show your shoe 84
shut your eyes 22
six pennies 87
skipping 69
snap the bacon 160
spanners 38
spit in the bucket 132
splits 85
stamp 134
stand and face your partner 115
stands a lady 103
stand to it 70
stand up 104
steadies 53, 62, 66
swing 11
tap-a-rap-a-rap-er 121
ten pennies 87
there grew an old apple tree 119
there's my black 103
there's my blue 103
this is the way 6; – she went 124, 125,
    126
thread a needle 163
three pennies 87
tick 28
tickle 134
tickly 6
tig 144
tip and tig 144
tip the ground 84
tippy 62
to-backy 62
tug of war 138, 141
turn it over 86
turn over 34, 89
turn your back 118
twirl around 84, 85
two pennies 87
umbrella 133
under the arch 63
under the moon 99
upstairs, downstairs 6
up the hill 63
up the ladder 88
walk straight out 50
we all fall down 12
we don't want 80
wibbly wobbly 86
wild man 25
yum, yum 163

INDEX

Affection and Fighting
army 18
bang 98, 113, 114, 115
bash 98
belt of the cane 122
black out 21
boxing 15
break every bone 75
break up 98
chop him up 98
clout 21, 150
creased 24
cut your throats 137
dear 123, 124
exploded 65
fell 56; – in 54; – out 54, 65; – over 56
fight 113, 115, 177; -ing 93
fire 113, 114, 115
flung him down 38
gun 65, 74
hang you 2
hit 66
hurt me 17
I'll chop you up in two 118
kick 67, 177; -ed 58
killed 24
kiss 18, 37, 94; -ing 169
knocked 150, 177
left them lying there 177
loaded 65
love(s) 69, 82, 89, 93, 103, 104, 175
lurry them up 177
massacred 24
poisoned 74, 75
pulled the trigger 65
punch 48
put her out 55
redden 2
rifles 109
rope 171
sacred life 2
scream 96
shake hands 6
sharpen 137
shoot 113, 114, 115
shout 59, 94
skelp 2
soldier(s) 2, 57, 90, 110, 111, 112, 113,
   114, 115, 126, 127
stole 6, 140, 150
stuck the knife in 171
swear 67
sweet 92

swore 75
threw 94, 97
trigger 65
war 110, 111, 113
whack 122
you'd run away with her 2
you'd steal her 2
you like the best 123

Age and Relationship
ashes 58
aunt(s) 72, 133
auntie 27
baby 28, 59, 89, 94, 111, 125, 150, 163,
   170, 171
baby brother 58, 76
birthday 49
born 74
boy(s) 37, 69, 79, 82, 93, 165, 169
brother 6, 58, 88
child(ren) 27, 54, 82, 91, 97, 102. 106,
   117
da 88
daddy 3, 5, 59, 94
daughter 110, 175
dead 15, 17, 76, 119, 163, 164, 166
die 11, 17, 23, 33, 54, 82, 92, 115, 117;
   -d 10, 51, 74, 125, 126
dust 58
family 97
father 2, 6, 59, 79, 123, 175
fellow 51, 92, 94
girl(s) 50, 69, 72, 75, 82, 93, 95, 96, 123,
   124
grandad 163, 164
grandmother 11
granny 3, 28, 161
grave 17
kids 98
lad 66
lady (ladies) 34, 54, 55, 64, 85, 97, 103,
   125, 126
life 175
little man 74
little sandy girls 81
love 80, 92, 116
ma 1, 60, 88
mademoiselle 78
maid 135, 136
ma'm 29
mammy 2, 3, 37, 56, 83, 89, 94
man 48, 98, 105, 106, 130, 131, 132, 133,

134, 137, 138, 142, 143, 146, 147,
148, 163, 164, 165, 166, 171; men
49
marry 80, 91, 92, 107, 108, 109, 110,
111, 112, 129; married 1, 55, 80, 92,
125
miss 57, 85
missus 16
mother(s) 16, 22, 27, 28, 48, 50, 55,
58, 59, 66, 67, 70, 74, 75, 76, 77, 82,
94, 122, 135, 136, 150, 165, 169, 175
offspring 106
old daddy 150
old granny 150
old man 73, 97
old one 167, 173
old woman 106, 119, 120, 170, 171
partner 123
people 50
sir 64, 107, 108, 109, 110
sister 65, 69, 79, 88, 174
sweetheart 18, 90, 92
three months old 170
uncles 133
wedding 55
wife 4, 77, 89, 93, 97, 102
woman 85
young 51; -man 103; -est child 117

Ailments, Cures and Injuries
back 94
baldy 15
bandy 16, 88
belly-ache 38, 172
blind 166
blisters 79
broken leg 166
chin 56
choked 37
cure 170
dummy 127
fail 150
fear 150
gumboil 172
hump 55
lip 59
mad 64
measles 55, 94
nervous 78
nose 54
oil 170
pain 170, 172
pimple 172
poisoned 74, 75

shy 174
sick 82
sting 163
suffer 17
tooth-ache 172
tumbled out 94
whooping-cough 55

Calls and Exclamations
ahem 21
all in, all in 146
am I in it 154, 155
calling out 49
caught ball eye o 67
cheer up . . . 177
cook 5
cowardy, cowardy, custard 15
follow all the way 152
game ball 173
good-bye 95, 106, 109
good morrow and good luck 18
good night 19, 84
I spy . . . 95, 96, 146, 163
I've no iron 145
lie all bars 152
no, no, no 163
oh, fie for shame 117
one, two, three, come out 146, 147
oo-ah, oo-ah, all the gang 147
open the gates 103
pax 144
please 50, 64, 84
Queenie eye o 67
ready, steady, go 70
relieve-ee-o 146
scut behind the car 25
scut the whip 25
sleep tight 19
stop 165
thank you 77
three cheers 59
up to me, up to me, 154
wrong spy 146
wrong spy eye o 147

Clothes
boots 91
buttons 33, 66
calico 163
cap 16
clogs 91
clothes 48, 92
coat 8, 95

182

INDEX

collar 22
dress 91, 106, 175; -ed 50, 75, 86, 96
golden slipper 131
hat 16, 95, 170
lace 10
lily-white bow 106
muslin 91
overcoat 150
pants 79, 173
peak 16
pocket(s) 1, 12, 14, 50, 116
rags 91
satin 91
shirt 9, 59, 171
shoe(s) 84, 91, 98, 148
silk 91, 175
slippers 73, 91
straw bamer 23
tall hat 74
umbrella 95
wool 31
wrap 163; -ed 94

Colours
black 21, 66, 75, 103, 107, 148, 171
blue 17, 50, 59, 86, 96, 103
colour 48, 65, 137; -s 73, 138
green 51, 75
lily-white 106
pink 52
red 137
rosie 12
white 51
yellow 48, 51, 65

Counting and Numbers
count 87
evens 130
first 85
five 40, 152, 163
five, six, seven, eight 54
five, ten, fifteen . . . hundred 10, 82, 91, 146, 148
four 49
four, five, six 57
nine 50
odds 130
one 10, 50
one, two, three 15, 23, 57, 58, 59, 70, 133, 146, 147
one, two, three, four 54
one . . . seven 5, 54
one . . . ten 153, 159
seven, eight, nine 57

sixteen 123
ten 57; – and ten 65
three(s) 10, 40, 171; – six nine 37
twenty 65
twenty-four 97, 163
two(s) 10, 19, 40, 49, 50, 75, 81, 171
two-a-bar 40
two to one 6

Division of Time
Days
Monday 82, 94, 98, 171
Monday . . . Sunday 135, 136
Saturday 63
Sunday 85, 98, 171
Tuesday 82, 94
Wednesday 82, 94

Months
January . . . December 91
November (19th of) 162

Time
afternoon 111
dark 87, 95, 96
day 175
forty years ago 56
fourteen days 75
half past eight 92, 96
half past one 149
half past three 80, 92
half past two 14, 98
morning 15, 75, 85, 121, 122; early in the –, 96, 120, 121
night 18, 63, 82, 172, 175
o'clock 143
one day 37
one o'clock 33, 149
to-day 131, 132
to-morrow 131, 132
week 59, 95

Entertainment and Recreation
band 127
dance 54, 55, 85, 116; -cing 124, 129
dargle 167
fiddle 6, 51, 117
fun 80
funny 87
gramophone 82
melodeon 15
play 51, 111, 150, 169; -ing 56, 165, 173
rodeo 60
sang 92

183

show 31
story 9
tune 51

Ethnic descriptions
black 55, 77
blackman 110
Chinese 50, 110
French 98, 158
German boys 87
Gipsy (gipsies) 57, **107, 111**
Highlander 2
Indian 12
Irish 59, 98
Jewman 75
nigger 164

Fauna
ass 91
beak 147
bee(s) 32, 163
birds 50
blackbirds 81
bugs 19
bumble-bee 32
bumbler 32
cat(s) 1, 22, 161
chicken 135, 136
cockle-shells 83
crow 18
dickie-birds 81
dog 11, 102
donkey 68, 125
duck(s) 18, 94, 150; -'s back 3
elephant 66, 71
fish(es) 50, 58, 176
flea(s) 59, 75
fox 24, 65, 71
gander 97
goose 37
heads 176
hen 3
horse 67, 174
kangaroo 17
ladybird 84
lark 87, 95, 96
monkey 37
mouse 123, 161
nanny-goat 5, 13
pig(s) 49, 50
piggy 7
pony 9
pussy 161
pussy-cat 17, 98

snake 38
sparrow 2
swans 111, 112
tails 176
tiger 65

Flora
apple(s) 9, 16, 37, 94, 119, 140, 144,
148, 161, 175; – tree 119
banana 56
bluebells 83, 120
buttercup 33
'chessers' 38
chestnuts 38
conker 38
daisy 33
dandelion 33
flowers 32, 72
fruit 73, 163
grass 64; green- 92
head of cabbage 133, **137**
Jinny-Joe 32
oil 170, 172
oranges 161
orchard 148
peach(es) 37, 49
pear(s) 37, 49, 94, 140, 160
plum(s) 49, 54
posies 12
'rhu-bob' 52
ripe 119
seasoner 38
straw 7
tobacco 37
trees 73
wallflowers 4, 117
woods 170, 171

Food, Drink and Cooking
apple jelly 90
apple pies 92
bacon 150, 160
barley-o 77
beef 89
beer 79
biscuit 66
boil 172; -ing 76, **79**
bone 6, 102
bottle 150
bread 15, 67, 75, 76, 161; – and butter
7; – and water 131
bun 14, 64
burned 81

184

butter 7, 29, 33, 61, 161
butts 22
cake 5, 111, 112, 113, 163
carmel rock 87
cayenne 78
chewed 37
chocolate(s) 57, 75, 76, 140
cocoa 15, 75
coffee 65
cool 74
cream 7
dinner 76, 149
dipped 58
drank 37
eat 58, 67, 96; – away 51; -ing 54, 57, 64
egg 32, 64, 122, 133
egg-shell 74
enarmel rock 87
feed 111, 172
fish 176
fresh 77
frying 81
ginger 78
glass 112, 113
glimmer 76
gruel 75
hams 29
head of cabbage 133, 137
hot 74
hot cross buns 97
ice cake 92
ice-cream 57, 86, 96, 140, 163
jam cake 92
jam pies 92
jams 29
jam-tart 90
jelly 86
kippers 73
leg of mutton 79
'lickerish' 77
licorice 77
loaf 49, 51, 172
marmalade 64
meat 6
mustard 15, 78
new milk 175
oatmeal 15
pancake(s) 74, 75
pepper 74, 75, 78
pie 21
pigs feet 49
porridge 15, 75

porter 50
potatoe(s) 5, 19
rasher 29, 122
ready 79
roast 74
salt 78
sausage(s) 81, 86
served 58
slice 113
sticky 77, 144
stout 150
sugar 15, 75, 76, 161
sugary candy 77, 87
swallowed 38, 65
sweets 29, 163
tea 29, 59, 61, 65, 77, 79, 92, 161
toast 64, 74
tossed 75
turned 75
vinegar 78
wine 37, 112, 113

House and Housekeeping
address 72
back-yard 173
bag 137
basket 62
bed 7, 15, 75, 76, 78, 171
blanket 34, 94
blue 14
bottle 12
box of colours 137
bucket 132
built 140
bundle of sticks 65
can 146
candle(s) 78, 163, 172
cane 122
chairs 98
chamber 97
chimney 74, 89, 150
chimney-pot 12
clappers 29
clean 108
comb 23, 34
cork 52
cradle 89
crochet 31
cup 21
dish 176
door 54, 80, 171
downstairs 97
fence 56, 66

fire-wood 98
floor 59, 86
fork 18
garden(s) 6, 19, 46, 50, 58, 136; – wall 150
gate(s) 96, 103
golden spoon 111
handle 169
home 3, 6, 7, 43, 94, 104, 135, 136
house 2, 27, 43, 86, 88
ink 52
ironing day 94
jam-jar 32
jelly-bag 62
kettle 79, 136
keys 112
kitchen 83
knife 18, 137, 171, 175
knit 106
ladder 88
lamp 18
letter-box 14
light 18, 84, 172
mangle 169
mirror 17
needle 163; – and thread 13
packet 64
pan 56, 81, 86, 117
penknife 171
pin 23, 31, 65, 175
plaster 98
plate 54, 86, 134
plough 18
po 31
pokers 107
pot 19
press 112
purses 64
razor 59
Rinso 64
scissors 132
sew 106, 137
shelf 75
soap 78
spout 88
stairs 1, 37, 38, 84, 94, 97 98
starch 14
steps 50
stick(s) 9, 17, 67, 98
stitching 83
tables 98
teacup 74
teapot 59, 88

telephone 77
television 143
tent 55, 123
tin can 73
towel 78
turpentine 57
T.V. 70, 77
umbrella 65, 133
upstairs 56, 97
wall, 81, 172
washed 57, 78
washes 92
wash her 175
washing 169; – day 94
weighing-scales 29
window 88
wiped 78
yard 59

Human Body
arse 1, 2
back 16, 55, 66, 75, 94
belly 3, 17, 67, 74, 170
blood 48
bone(s) 12, 17, 75
bum 57, 74, 172
chin 56
eye(s) 3, 11, 17, 22, 59, 92, 123, 174
face 17, 137
fart 67
feet 1, 2, 49, 79, 80, 91, 161
finger(s) 131, 163
foot 131, 132, 148; left – 66; right – 66
forehead 3
hair 18, 57
hand(s) 2, 6, 34, 36, 78, 106, 109, 123, 124, 175
head 15, 76, 141, 163, 171
heart 171
heel(s) 1, 54, 55
hips 124
left side 172
leg(s) 15, 34, 65, 88; left – 61, 64, 97; right – 61, 64
lip 59
mouth(s) 2, 22
neck 79, 171
nose 10, 12, 48, 54, 88
shins 177
shoulder 121
spit 132
stink 52
throats 137

toe(s) 54, 55, 88, 163
whiskers 79, 174

Letters and Spelling
A.B 163
A-Z 75, 76, 90, 164
d.i.f.f.i.c.u.l.t.y 37
d.o.n.k.e.y 68
G.O go 71, 87, 95, 96
G.P.O. 55
H 76
K 166
M.A.Y.P.O.L.E 61
O.U.T 54, 71, 76, 77
X.Y 50
X.Y.Z 15, 75, 76
y.o.u 107, 108, 109, 110

Locations of Games
aeroplane beds 157
alley-o 162, 163, 169
arrow 145
beds 153
den 146, 147
French beds 158
ground 84
highway 129
lamp-post 64, 72, 148
lane 52
mowl 38
name beds 155, 156
'rest' bed 154
roundy beds 156
street(s) 37, 80, 92
town 13, 65
traffic lights 131
village 115

Minerals
gold 103, 175
iron 145
lead 67
marble 92
silver 66, 103

Money and Commerce
bought 51, 64, 67
business 18
buy 15, 58, 70, 77; – away 29
eighteen pence 51
eight pennies 87
eleven pennies 87
fair 72

fardel 167
farthing 58, 106, 109
five pennies 87
four pennies 87
four yards 9
half a crown 21
ha'penny 14, 65, 172
loan 117
lump 96
market 7, 161
money 29, 50, 86, 87, 112
nine pennies 87
one and four 49
one and nine 67
one a penny 97
one penny 87
pay my fare 97
pence 56
penny 15, 96
pension 59
piece 77, 111, 112
pound (weight) 49, 89
pounds 56
rent 55
sell 67
seven pennies 87
shilling(s) 56, 87, 173
sixpence 37, 94
six pennies 87
sixty cents 66
ten pennies 87
three ha'pence 16, 176
three pennies 87
threepenny bit 49
tuppence 14, 16, 59
twenty cents 37, 64
two a penny 97
two pennies 87

Nature and Elements
cold and frosty 121, 122
east 123
fine weather 95, 96
frosty 13
frozen 10
lake 38, 111, 112
noon 12
mountain 103
north, south, east, west 76
rain 21; – blew high 92
rainbow 63
river 92, 170, 171
sand 137

sea 50, 58, 72, 77
sea-shore 81
sky 56, 66, 92, 110
stars 12
stones 12, 17, 169
thunder 67
very fine day 110
water 3, 22, 131, 150; across the – 131, 132
well 22, 78
west 123
wind blew high 110
wind blows 13
windy weather 13
world 2

Nonsense Refrains and Repetitive Phrases
a baa booshalom 49, 50
a nailey-o 6
a-rover : rick-a-rock . . .
a-sha, a-sha 12
barbel-ee, barbel-o 6
bissa bonka : issa . . .
bum, bum, bailey-o 6
can-ika, swim-ika 173
cheer boys cheer 169
claimy clappy 62
clainy clappy 62
cock-cock-a-rooshy 131
dicky dicky dout 9
dilly dally 165
ding dong dell 137
drip, drop 72, 77
echo, echo 71, 87, 95, 96
ee eye 119, 120
ee eye, ee eye 102
ee eye o 109
eena meena 49
ee-ver, eye-ver 83, 89
give-ika, you-ika 173
goosey goosey gander 97
grunt, grunt, grunt 7
gummy gummy goo 14
haw, haw . . . 124
hick, hack 38
hippety hop 120
hippy tippy 62
I die didily i 78
if-ika, you-ika 173
I-ika, will-ika 173
issa bissa bonka 50
li-ika, my-ika 173
lone-y, lone-y 9

loop-ee-o 71, 72, 77
maggoty daw : see-saw . . .
meena : eena . . .
pish, wish, wish 161
plainy clappy 62
plonk-plonk 31
quack, quack, quack 94
relieve-ee-o 169
rick-a-rock-a-rover 89
rick stick stelly 17
rick stick stoil 17
rick stick stoor 17
rolley to-backy 62
see-saw maggoty daw 7
son-ika, John-ika 173
spin, spout 21
swing, swong, sway 10, 11
tap-a-rap-a-rap-er 121
tick-tack, tick-tack 98
tick-tack-too 98
tippy : hippy . . .
tippy teena 49, 50
tra la la la la 110
vote, vote, vote 80
weel-ya, weel-ya, wall-ya 170, 171
wibbly wobbly 86
yip, yip 5, 13
yum, yum 163

Occupations
army 18
baker 2, 66, 165
barber 16, 18, 59
beggar 135; -man 83, 90
bride 16
butcher 89, 136
chimney sweeper 89
cobbler 8, 98
digging a ditch 18
doctor(s) 15, 76, 77, 82, 95, 170
earl 3
farmer 4, 102, 123
girl guide 86
governor 110
horseman 174
inspector 97
Irish soldiers 112, 113
king 8, 35, 109
landlord 55
Lord Mayor 16, 173
master(s) 98, 121, 135, 136
mend my shoe 98
nun 14, 64

nurses 64, 95
officer 86
policeman 97, 127, 171
Polony man 128
postman 57, 96
queen 75, 86, 106, 124
red rover 139
robber(s) 86, 136, 140
Roman soldiers 113, 114, 115
sailor(s) 58, 72, 77, 90, 127
shaved 59
soldier(s) 2, 57, 90, 110, 111, 126, 127
tailor 90
teacher 28, 125
thief 90
tinker 90
washerwoman 126
waxies 167
working hard 59

Personal Descriptions
Unfavourable Nouns
baa 1
bag of cats 1
baldy-conscience 15
baldy nopper 15
baldy-peelo 15
baldy-sconce 15
bandy-legs 88
big fat pussy-cat 17
boor 17
bugger 2
canat 2
cap of apples 16
cowardy custard 15
crab 2
faggot 2
farthing-face 2
ferret 2
fool 19
get 2, 3
get of hell 2
grannuaile 2
heart-scald 2
hoor 17
jackass 19
ma's plaster 1
melodeon legs 15
ninety-eight and boney 2
ninety-eight in the shade 2
poor man 90
rascal 35
rogue 6

scut 2, 3
skinnymalink 15
sleeveen get 2
slut 7
sparrow-fart 2
specky-four-eyes 15
star of hope 3
starve the barber 16
steps of stairs 1
sugar babby 15
tell-tale tattler 15
whinge 1

Unfavourable Adjectives
bad 64
baldy 15, 71
baldy-headed 98
bandy 16
cockeyed 16
crabby 2
dirty 55, 107, 108
ferrety-faced 2
full of fat 74
gummy 15
lazy 121
marble eye 92
poor 106, 109
small 67
stiff 107
teapot nose 88
turned in toes 88
turned up nose 88

Favourable Nouns
bunser 3
chickies 163
chum 49
fairest one 109
fair lady 140
fair maid(s) 117, 129
granny hen 3
little hen 3
pretty maid 129
rich man 90

Favourable Adjectives
bonny 69, 82
brave 110, 111
clean 55
conny 2
fairest 106
handsome 92
long-legged 58

nice 102, 103
strong 110, 111
pretty 92, 117, 163
tall 67

Personal Names
Standard
Anne 123, 124
Annie Oakley 70, 77
Auntie Mary 57
Billy 18, 59
Billy Boland 66
Bob 52
Cadbury's 76
Caroline 57
Charlie Chaplain 54, 55, 85
Daddy Aiken 150
Dan 73
De Valera 80
Dick Mc Clane 8
Dicky 9
Doctor Doyle 170
Doctor Kelly 170
Doctor Moore 170
Doctor Wyatt 170
Dolly 64
Doyle 17
Eileen 65
Esau 76
Garret Reilly 3
Granny Grey 150
Handy Andy 87
Jack 35, 43, 74, 75, 118
Janey Mac 171
Jinny 13, 54, 77
John 88, 173
Johnny 37, 65, 94, 131, 132
Johnston Mooney & O'Brien 67
Judy 10
Kelly 17
Kennedy 67
Lyons 70, 77
Mary 121, 123, 169
Mary Anne 12, 56, 123
Mary Mac 66
Mary Murphy 123
Maypole 61
Merville Dairy 57
Michael 88
Minnie 65
Molly 46
Moore 17
Mr. Flynn 56

Mr. Fox 149
Mrs. Bates 56
Mrs. Brown 65
Mrs. Dunne 64
name(s) 7, 17, 85, 155, 156, 175; -ed 81
Nellie 55
O'Grady 160
Old Roger 119
O'Leary 57
Paddy 5, 12
Paul 81
Peter 81
Punch and Judy 10
Rosie 9
Sally 12, 133
Sister Eithne 95
Tim 65
Tom 164
Woolworths 143

Nicknames
Burr'ner 16
Jemser 16
Johnny Magory 9
Johnny Wetbread 8
Mickser 16
Padser 16
Paddy whack 16
Proddy Woddy 172
Queenie 57, 67
Redser 16
Smither 16
Whacker 16
Willie Wagtail 74

Place Names
Standard
Ballybough Bridge 66
Bow Lane 140
Caroline 37
China 58
Cole's Lane 7
Cork 166
country (countries) 73, 129
Derry 166
Dirty Lane 7, 8
Dublin 115, 121, 166; – city 93
Finglas 94
France 54, 55, 85, 173
Germany 58
Greece 58
Hungary 58
Italy 58

Japan 58
Kerry 166
London 34
Mediterranean Sea 58
Nelson's Pillar 83
O'Connell St. 49
Paris 173
Sandy Land 106
Sicily 58
Turkey 58
U.S.A. 165
Wicklow 142

Nicknames
Brunner 16
Croker 16
Dalyier 16
Norrier 16
Punchardstown 174

Public Buildings
baker's shop 165
castle 35, 140
chapel 9
chipper 16
church 91, 104
convalescent home 95
cottage 54
G.P.O. 55
hall 111
hospital 94
Penny Bazaar 60
public house 50, 79
school 74, 75, 98, 124
shop(s) 29, 37, 67

Religion and Superstition
amen 49
April fool 19
Ash Wednesday 74
bad angel 138
banshee 1, 23
before you die 23
bible 172
christened 74
crying someone out of the house 23
devil 58, 59, 138
down below 19
fairy 65, 75
forgiven 54
ghost 64, 136
God 1, 19, 22, 58, 98; – 's pocket 1
good angel 137

good luck 23
grace 52
Hail Mary 52
heaven 33, 37, 54, 59, 134, 138
hell 2, 6, 33, 59, 67, 134, 138; – 's gates 2
lie 71
limbo 33
lucky place 52
Mass 98
mercy 177
paradise 59
prayers 78, 84, 97, 104
prays (to God) 98
purgatory 33
redemption 59
Shrove Tuesday 74, 75
sins 54
Sunday 98
unlucky eye 2
witch 65, 148

Riches
gold 103, 175
gold band 106
golden ball 111
golden crown 131
golden ring 131
golden slipper 131
golden spoon 111
plenty 65
rich 18, 65
ring 104
silver 66, 103
watch and chain 140

School
arithmetic 98
call the roll 82
ecker 16
holidays 13
holliers 16
letter 116
master 98
pen and ink 176
reading 98
school 74, 75, 98, 124; – bench 98
stick 98
taught 54
teach 54, 55, 85, 98
write 175; writing 98

Toys
badges 33

ball 67, 159, 161
chalk 44
chanies 29
comb and paper 34
cords 31
five slates 39
golden ball 111
hoop 46
jackers 16, 40
jackstones 16, 39
jam-jar 32
lash 44, 45
marbles 151
match-box 32
meat-skewer 31
nail 30, 31
peep-show 31
pickey 45, 153
rattler 15
rope 25, 72, 77, 89
see-saw 76
shoe-box 31
silver paper 34
spool 31
steeler 16, 151
stilts 30
stones 39
swing 10

taw 151
teddy bear 6, 84
tins 30
top 44
wheel 47

Vehicles and Transport
aeroplane 157
ambulance 22
ass and cart 91
big ship 162
bike 63
boat 83
carriage(s) 82, 91, 175
C.I.E. 97
coach 91
deck 79
dung-cart 74
engine 12
fairy-bike 63
horse and car 60
pram 94
railway 5, 12
riding 107
rowing boat 37
sailed 58
two-wheeler 63

A-b-c-d-e-f-g 75, 76
A boy stood on a burning deck 79
All around the village 115
All in, all in* 146
All in together girls* 95, 96
Amen means 'so be it' 49
A pig went into a public house 50
A pin to see the show 31
Apple jelly my jam-tart* 90
April fool is dead and gone 19
April fool is gone past 19
Are you the lad 66
Ashes to ashes 58
Ash Wednesday, Shrove Tuesday* 74
As I went up some Chinese steps* 50
A tinker, a tailor 90
At the dirty end of dirty lane 8

Baby's eyes are Irish 59
Bad angel, bad angel 138
Beg your pardon 19
Billy Boland 66
Billy the barber 59
Billy with the lamp 18
Bluebells, cockle-shells* 83
Bum, bum, bailey-o 6
Buy away, buy away* 29

Charlie Chaplin 85
Charlie Chaplin went to France*
54, 55
Chase, chase, chase the baldy
elephant 71
Cheer boys cheer* 169
Cheer up 'Sycamore'* 177
Chinese Governor 110
Clap hands, clap hands 5
Cobbler, cobbler, mend my shoe 98
Cowardy, cowardy, custard 15

Dancing up the highway* 129
Dear Anne, dear Anne 123
Dicky, dicky, dout 9
Die, die, little dog die* 11
Dolly, Dolly, had no sense 64
Don't eat Kennedy's bread 67
Down by the river* 92
Down in Nelson's Pillar 83
Down in the alley-o* 169
Doyle, the boil 17
Drip, drop, dropping in the sea* 72
Drip, drop, the sailors on the sea
72, 77
Dublin, Derry, Cork and Kerry 166

Each a peach a pear a plum 49

Early in the morning* 96
Eena, meena 49, 50
Ee-ver, eye-ver, chimney sweeper*
89

Five, ten, fifteen, twenty 10

German boys are not so funny 87
Gipsy, gipsy, Caroline 57
Give a thing 19
Going around the garden* 58
Going, going 147
Good angel, good angel 137
Good night, sleep tight 19
Goosey goosey gander 97
Green, white, and yellow 51
Gummy, gummy, goo 14

Hail Mary full of grace 52
Half of the castle is built, built 140
Handy Andy sugary candy 87
Have a piece of barley-o* 77
Here comes the bride 16
Here's the gipsy riding, riding, rid-
ing 107
Here's the King arriving, arriving,
arriving 109
Here's the old woman from Sandy
Land* 106
Here's the robbers passing by* 140
He's baldy from boxing 15
Hide and go seek 147
Hop, hop, to the baker's shop* 165
Hot cross buns 97
How is your old one* 173

I call in my sister 69
Ice-cream a penny a lump 96
If a gumboil could boil oil 172
If-ika you-ika can-ika swim-ika 173
If you can swim like my son John
172
I had a box of chocolates 75
I have a gumboil* 172
I know an old woman who lived in
the woods* 170
I know a woman* 85
I'll tell you a story 9
I made you look 18
I'm a little girl guide 86
I'm a soldier brave and strong* 110
I'm looking at you 17
I'm stirring my chicken, my chicken
my chicken 135, 136
I'm the king of the rifles, rifles,
rifles 109

I'm the king of the castle 35
I'm the wee Polony man* 128
In and out through the darkie blue-
bells* 120
Ink a pink 52
Inspector, inspector, don't take me
97
In the dirty end of Dirty Lane 8
. . . is a very good man 98
I saw Esau 76
I scream, you scream 96
I see Paris 173
I sent a letter to my love* 116
. . . is no good 98
I think, I think 52
I've a bike* 63
I've a pain in my belly 170

Janey Mac 171
Jelly on a plate 86
Jinny go up 13
Jinny on the telephone 77
Johnny gave me apples 37
Johnny had a gun 65
Johnny may I go across the water?
131, 132
Johnston Mooney and O'Brien 67

Keep it boiling 76
Keep the kettle boiling* 79
Kelly, the belly 17
K is for Kathleen 163

Lazy Mary, will you get up* 121
Little black doctor 77
Little Mary in her tent 123
Little Nellie in her tent* 55
Long-legged Italy 58
Long or short 165
Look who's coming down the street
80

Mademoiselle 78
Ma, let's go* 60
Mary Anne 56
Mary Mac, Mac, Mac 66
Maypole butter, maypole tea 61
Mind your own business 18
Minnie the witch 65
Molly I'd love to be rolling your
hoop* 46
Monday is my washing day 94
Monday night the gramophone* 82
Money on the floor 86
Moore, the boor 17
Mother, mother, I feel sick 82

Mr. Flynn 56
Mrs. Browne 65
Mrs. D. Mrs. I 37
Mrs. Dunne made her bun 64
My mammy said 56
My mammy sent me to the shops
one day 37
My mother and your mother 48
My mother, my mother 55
My sister Eileen and I fell out 65
My straw bamer, one, two, three 23

No more Irish 98
No one can come out of hell 59

Oh! the horse broke down* 174
Oo-ah, oo-ah* 147
Old Daddy Aiken 150
Old Granny Grey* 150
Old Roger is dead and he lies in his
grave* 119
Once I had the measles 94
One potatoe 5
One, two, three 59
One two, three, four 54
One, two, three, four, five, six,
seven 54
One, two, three O'Leary* 57
Oosha Mary Murphy 123
Our school is a very good school 98

Paddy on the railway* 12
Paddy whack 16
Plainy, clappy, rolley, to-backy 62
Plainy marmalade 64
Plainy packet of Rinso 64
Please get off the grass, Sir 64
Policeman, policeman, don't take
me* 97
Pounds, shillings and pence 56
Pie, pie, come out 21
Proddy woddy on the wall 172
Punch and Judy ran a race 10

Queenie eye-o 67

Rain, rain, come down 21
Ring-a-ring-a-rosie* 12
Robbers in the house 86
Rosie apple, went to chapel 9
Round and round the garden 6
Round apple, round apple* 175

Sally go round the moon 12
Salt, mustard, ginger, cayenne 78
Sausage on the pan 86

194

INDEX OF FIRST LINES

Says my old one* 167
See a pin 23
See-saw, maggoty daw 7
. . . sells fish 176
Shake hands brother 6
Shake the blanket* 34
Shrove Tuesday, Shrove Tuesday 75
Shut your eyes 22
Somebody under the bed* 78
Stands a lady, on the mountain*
    103, 104
Sticks and stones 17
Sugar babby, sugar babby 15
Supposing, supposing 10

Teddy bear, teddy bear* 84
Tell-tale tattler 15
Ten and ten are twenty 65
The big ship sails through the alley,
    alley o 162
The boy stood on the burning deck
    79
The farmer wants a wife* 102
The rain, the rain* 92
There was a girl in our school* 124
There was a little man 74
There was an old man* 73
This is the way my father showed
    me 6
This little piggy went to the market
    7
Three, six, nine 37
Tiger Tim 65

Two little dickie-birds* 81
Two little fleas 75
Two little sandy girls 81
Two little sausages 81
Two potatoes in a pot 19

Up the ladder, down the spout* 88
Up to me, up to me, never get
    apast me 154

Vote, vote, vote* 80

Wallflowers, wallflowers* 117
What's your name? 7
When I die 17
When I was a washerwoman, a
    washerwoman, a washerwoman*
    126
When I was young* 51
Where are you going Bob? 52
Willie Willie Wagtail 74
Will you have a glass of wine?* 112
Windy weather* 13

X-Y-Z 15

Yellow, yellow 65
Yip, yip, a nanny-goat 13
You're in the army now 18

* denotes inclusion of music